LITERACY
>POWER

- HEROES
- GETTING THE MESSAGE
- IDENTITY
- MEDIA
- BODY SCIENCE
- CHALLENGES

gagelearning

National Library of Canada Cataloguing in Publication
Main entry under title: Literacy power: book F
ISBN 0-7715-1048-9

English language—Textbooks

LB1631.L579 2003 428   C2003-903832-7

Any Web sites visited through www.gagelearning.com have been checked for appropriate content. However, these Web sites and any other suggested links should be periodically checked before the addresses are given to students. Web addresses change constantly. Teachers should locate the URL through a search engine, and check the site for appropriate content.

Care has been taken to trace ownership of copyright material contained in this text. The publishers will gladly take any information that will enable them to rectify any reference or credit in subsequent editions.

We wish to thank all the teachers, consultants, and students across Canada who contributed feedback during the development of this series.

We acknowledge the financial support of the Government of Canada through the Book Publishing Industry Development Program for our publishing activities.

We acknowledge the Government of Ontario through the Ontario Media Development Corporation's Ontario Book Initiative.

Production: Loretta Mah
Researcher: Catherine Rondina
Permissions: Elizabeth Long
Design: First Image
Cover Photo: Getty Images/Mike Powell

ISBN 0-7715-1048-9
1 2 3 4 5 MP 07 06 05 04 03
Written, printed, and bound in Canada

Acknowledgments **2-3** "What Is a Hero?" © Gage Learning Corporation, 2003; **7-9** "Joseph Jackson: An Impossible Strength" from *Kid Heroes* by Neal Shusterman (New York: Lowell House/RGA Publishing Group, Inc., 1991). Reprinted with permission of the author; **14-15** "How to Save Someone Who Is Hanging From a Cliff" from *The Action Hero's Handbook* by David Borgenicht and Joe Borgenicht (Philadelphia, PA: Quirk Productions Inc., 2002); **19-21** "Against the Jungle" by Steve Lawton, © Gage Learning Corporation, 2003; **28-29** "The Way of a Winner" by Jesse Marcel Bruneau from *Courageous Spirits: Aboriginal Heroes of Our Children* edited by Joann Archibald, Val Friesen, and Jeff Smith (Penticton, BC: Theytus Books, 1993); **33** "O Siem" by Susan Aglukark and Chad Irschick from *This Child*, CD, ©Aglukark Entertainment Inc.; **37-39** "Tell the World" from *Tell the World* by Severn Cullis-Suzuki. Reprinted with permission of the author; **43-44** "Whoever Said Don't Run…" Bully Issue Card by permission of Kids Help Phone; **50-51** "Stupid Things I Did to be Cool" © 2001 by Consumers Union of U.S., Inc., Yonkers, NY 10703-1057, a non-profit organization. Reprinted with permission from Zillions®: Consumer Reports® for Kids Web site for educational purposes only. No commercial use or photocopying permitted. Log on to www.Zillions.org; **53-54** "Skate Secrets." Copyright © 1989 Caleen Sinnette Jennings. Reprinted from *A Lunch Line: Contemporary Scenes for Contemporary Teens* by permission of New Plays Incorporated, Charlottesville, VA 22905; **57-60** "What's Your Learning Style?" Excerpted from *Psychology for Kids I: 40 Fun Tests That Help You Learn About Yourself* by Jonni Kincher © 1995. Used with permission from Free Spirit Publishing Inc., Minneapolis, MN; 1-866-703-7322, www.freespirit.com. All rights reserved; **63-64** "Message Mix-Ups" by Diane Robitaille © Gage Learning Corporation, 2003; **68** "Yesterday" a selection from *Hey World, Here I Am!* written by Jean Little and illustrated by Sue Truesdale, used by permission of Kids Can Press Ltd., Toronto. Text copyright © 1986 by Jean Little; **74-75** "E-Communications Time line" from *Internet Electronic Global Village* by David Jefferis (St. Catharines, ON: Crabtree Publishing Company, 2002), © 2002 David Jefferis/Alpha Communications; **80-81** "Teens Logon to Stay Connected," (originally "YTV Kid and Tween Report, 2001, Wave 7.") YTV is a registered trademark of Corus Entertainment Inc. Reprinted with permission; **81** "Web Safety" © (2003) HER MAJESTY THE QUEEN IN RIGHT OF CANADA as represented by the Royal Canadian Mounted Police (RCMP). Reprinted with the permission of the RCMP; **83** "Zits" cartoon strip (2/6/03) © Zits Partnership. Reprinted with Special Permission of King Features Syndicate; **85-87** "Behind the Scenes with a TV Tester" (originally "Behind the Scenes with Goody Germer") from *The TV Book: The Kid's Guide to Talking Back* by Shelagh Wallace (Toronto: Annick Press Ltd., 1996) © 1996 Shelagh Wallace; **91** "How Much TV Are Canadians Watching?" adapted from the Statistics Canada Web site, http://www.statcan.ca/Daily/English/021202/d021202a.htm, January 29, 2003. *Statistics Canada information is used with the permission of the Minister of Industry, as Minister responsible for Statistics Canada. Information on the availability of the wide range of data from Statistics Canada can be obtained from Statistics Canada's Regional Offices, its World Wide Web site at http://www.satcan.ca, and its toll-free access number 1-800-263-1136*; **97-98** "The Human Body" from *Factastic Book of 1001 Lists* by Russell Ash © 1999 Dorling Kindersley Limited, London; text © 1999, 1998 Russell Ash; **101-103** "A Better Backpack for Your Back" © 2000 by Consumers Union of U.S., Inc. Yonkers, NY 10703-1057, a non-profit organization. Reprinted with permission from Zillions®: Consumer Reports® for Kids Web site for educational purposes only. No commercial use or photocopying permitted. Log onto www.Zillions.org; **108-110** "Chills, Thrills, and Spills" by Samantha Bonar from *Owl* Magazine (Summer 1999), pp. 10-12; **114-116** "Life in a Bubble" from *The Book of You* by Sylvia Funston (Toronto: Owl Books, 2000). Text © 2000 Sylvia Funston. Owl Books are published by Maple Tree Press; **119-122** "The Art of Optical Illusions" from *The Art of Optical Illusions* by Al Seckel. A Carlton Book. Text and illustrations © Illusion Works 2000 with the exception of p. 121 (bottom) © Nicholas Wade; **126-128** "A Small Victory" (originally "Haven Small") by William Joyce from *Tikvah: Children's Book Creators Reflect on Human Rights* (Storrs-Mansfield, Connecticut: The University of Connecticut, 1999). Reprinted with permission of the University of Connecticut; **133-134** "The 'Man in the Family' Is Just a Boy" by Alan Freeman (Toronto: The Globe and Mail, 2001). Reprinted with permission from *The Globe and Mail*; **137-139** "How to Write a Petition" from *Take Action! A Guide to Active Citizenship* by Marc Kielburger and Craig Kielburger, © Gage Learning Corporation, 2002; **143-147** "The Vigil" by Jan Andrews. Reprinted with permission of the author.

Photo Credits **2 (left; middle)** Everett Collection/MAGMA; **2 (right)** Charles Fiddler; **3 (top)** CP PHOTO/*Toronto Star*/Rick Madonik; **3 (middle)** CP PHOTO/Scott Audette; **3 (Bottom)** CP PHOTO/Glenn Asakawa; **15** © *Tom Stewart/CORBIS*; **33** Pierre Tremblay/Masterfile; **37** Barbara Woodley; **109** CP/PA PHOTO/Toby Melville; **110** CP PHOTO/*Toronto Star*/Peter Power; **115** © 2000 Gilbert Ducas; **121 (bottom)** © Nicholas Wade; **133** © Thomas HEGANBART (AGENTUR FOCUS/CONTACT PRESS IMAGES).

Illustrations **8-9, 28-29, 63-64** Tyrone McCarthy/3 in a Box; **19-21** Steve Lawton/Air Hero's Studio; **38-39** illustrations courtesy the students of the Etobicoke School of the Arts and Central Technical School, Ontario, Canada; **53-54** Dominic Bugatto/3 in a Box; **74-75** Oksana Kemarskaya/Oksana Kemarskaya Illustration; **86** Noel Tuazon/Noel Tuazon Illustration and Design; **137, 139** Stephen MacEachern; **143, 145, 147** Emma Barkworth/Emma Barkworth Illustration.

TABLE OF CONTENTS

HEROES

GETTING THE MESSAGE

*indicates Canadian content

Alternate Table of Contents

Before Reading

Who do you think of when you hear the word **hero**? _____

Why? _____

What Is a HERO?

DICTIONARY DEFINITION WITH QUOTATIONS from Various Authors

he•ro (hë-rö) *n, pl* **he•roes.** –**he•roic,** *adj*
1 a person who is greatly admired for his or her courage, leadership, strength, or skill. **2** the most important character in a story, play, or movie

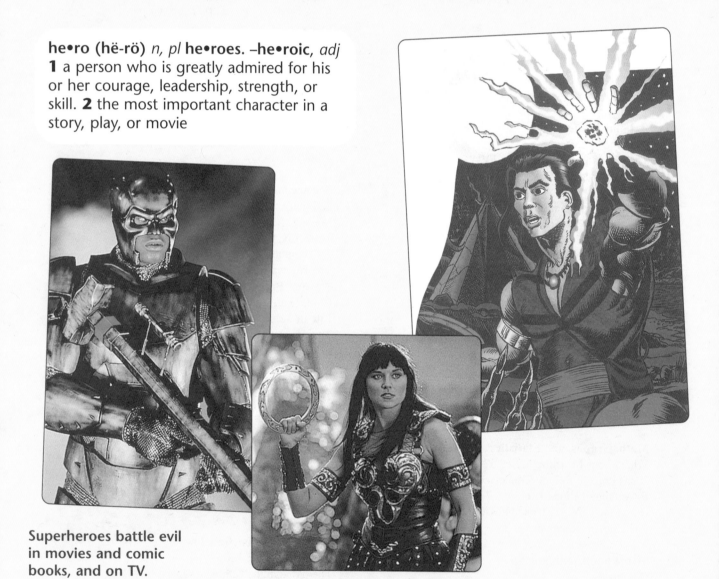

Superheroes battle evil in movies and comic books, and on TV.

GOALS AT A GLANCE

thinking about meaning • using the dictionary

1 "We can never be certain of our courage until we have faced danger."
— **La Rochefoucauld**

2 "Courage is not the absence of fear, but rather the judgment that something else is more important than fear."
— **Ambrose Redmoon**

3 "Great opportunities to help others seldom come, but small ones surround us every day."
— **Sally Koch**

4 "To go against the **dominant** [popular or widespread] thinking of your friends…is perhaps the most difficult act of heroism you can perform."
— **Theodore H. White**

These heroes face real-life challenges.

UNDERSTANDING THE SELECTION *Thinking About Meaning*

1. Match each quotation on page 3 with one of the following statements. Write the number of the quotation in the space provided.

   a. People have lots of chances to be heroes in small ways. _____

   b. Sometimes being a hero means standing up for your beliefs. _____

   c. Courage is doing things you think important even though you are afraid. _____

   d. You can't know how brave you are until you face a dangerous situation. _____

2. Which quotation is the most meaningful to you? _____ Explain your choice. _____

   _____

EXTENDING: In your notebook, write a statement about heroes or courage.

B

VOCABULARY *Using the Dictionary*

> A **dictionary** is a book of words listed in alphabetical order with their meanings.
> - The **entry word** shows you the spelling of a word and divides it into syllables.
> - The **pronunciation key** tells you how to say the word.
> - The **definition** tells you the meanings of the word.
> - **Special forms** show how the word can be used in different ways (as an adverb or adjective, for example) and how the spelling may change.

1. On page 2, label the parts of the dictionary entry for the word **hero**. Use the following labels: **entry word**, **pronunciation**, **special forms**, **definitions**.
2. Here is a sample sentence for the **first** definition of the word **hero**:
   The firefighter's daring rescue of the young boy makes her a real hero in our home town.
   Write a sample sentence for the **second** definition of the word **hero**.

   _____

   _____

3. Look up **hero** in at least **two** dictionaries and read the definitions.
4. How did looking up **hero** in different dictionaries add to your understanding of the word?

   _____

   _____

   _____

Reflecting

LANGUAGE CONVENTIONS *Nouns*

> • A **noun** is a word that names a person, place, thing, event, or idea.
>   EXAMPLES: courage, danger, friends, hero, story, school, holidays, chair

1. Underline each noun in the following sentences. The number of nouns in each sentence is indicated in brackets.

   a. Opportunities to help other people seldom come along. (2)

   b. Redmoon says, "Courage is not the absence of fear…." (4)

   c. My sister and brother saw Gretzky play in Edmonton. (4)

   d. On Halloween, my friends invited me to a party. (3)

> • A **proper noun** names a **particular** person, place, event, or thing. Proper nouns begin with capital letters.
>   EXAMPLES: Adriana is a hero to all of us here at Green Forest High School
>   ever since she won the Carnegie Medal of Honour last New Year's Day.

2. Rewrite each of the following sentences. Replace the underlined nouns with proper nouns. Hint: sometimes, you'll also have to replace the word that comes before the noun for your new sentence to make sense.

   a. My teacher drives a car to school every day.

   _____

   b. My friend doesn't live in this city.

   _____

   c. My sister read this book too.

   _____

   d. That province is right next to my province.

   _____

3. Write **two** sentences about a person you think is a hero. Underline any nouns in your sentences. Circle any proper nouns.

   _____

   _____

During Reading
"Joseph Jackson: An Impossible Strength"

"Joseph Jackson: An Impossible Strength" is a true account of a heroic rescue. Read and think about the questions in the chart below. As you read the true account, record your answers to these questions.

Questions	Answers
1. Who was involved in the accident?	
2. Where did the accident happen?	
3. What happened exactly?	
4. Why is Joseph Jackson a hero?	
5. How did Joseph feel after the accident?	

Reading With a Purpose

Whenever you start to read a new text, think about your **purpose**. Sometimes you read to get information. Sometimes you read for enjoyment. Read this text to find out what happened to Joseph and why he was a hero.
- Read the headings for each section first. The headings will help you figure out where information is located.
- Read each section, and then stop to think about the information in it.
- Look at the above questions after each section to see if you can answer them.
- Use the information in the pictures to help you.

Joseph Jackson: An Impossible Strength

TRUE ACCOUNT by Joseph Jackson and Neal Shusterman from *Kid Heroes*

BEFORE THE ACCIDENT

It happened like this…we were moving out to Virginia, and our Bronco was loaded right to the roof with everything we owned. I rode up front with Mom, and my cousin Billy rode in the very back. Around him we had packed everything under the sun. The Bronco was packed solid. We were taking a shortcut to our new home, going down a narrow, winding gravel road. Lately we'd been having a lot of trouble with the Bronco. It would rev up really fast and then cut down, and then it would kick in really fast again without any warning.

THE ACCIDENT

We were going about 50 km/h around this curve when the Bronco went out of control. We swerved to the other side of the road, came back, hit a bridge, and flew right off the bridge, into the water.

The water was deep, because beavers had dammed up the river below. Mom's window was down, and as the car hit the water, we tipped, and water began to gush in. We were <u>submerging</u> fast! In a second, we were completely underwater. My Mom, who can't swim, was choking and gasping as the water filled her lungs.

Ask Yourself
If you were Joseph, what would you be thinking right now?

GOALS AT A GLANCE

identifying main events • drawing conclusions

THE RESCUE

That's when I rammed my fist through my window to break it. I pulled Mom over, and out the window. I don't know how I was able to do it, but I did. She was choking and coughing when we broke surface, completely out of it, and I swam with her to shore.

The slippery riverbank was steep, and it was hard to get her up there, but somehow it was like I suddenly had superhuman strength or something, and I pushed her up. I really don't know how I was able to do it!

It wasn't until then that I realized I had a deep gash on my wrist, and it was bleeding badly. Then it dawned on me that my ten-year-old cousin Billy was still in the car, completely blocked in!

"I got to get Billy, I got to get Billy," I screamed and went back into the water, swimming toward the submerged car. I stuck my hand into the car, opened the door, and had to unpack the whole back seat to get to Billy. Everything under the sun was stuffed in around him. I thought I'd never get to him. Finally, I found him, carried him out, and brought him over to the shore. He had a bad bruise, but was okay.

Before the Accident

The Accident

This **sequence diagram** shows the major events in this true account. (Notice how this diagram looks a lot like a comic strip. Most comic strips relate a sequence of events, too!)

AFTER THE RESCUE

My aunt, grandfather, and brother were up at the bridge. They'd been driving way ahead of us, but heard the crash and came back. Now that it was over, I was pretty shaky, and losing blood fast. My aunt came down, took off her blouse, and wrapped it around my wrist to stop the bleeding. Then they rushed us all over to the hospital. They stitched my wrist up all right, but because the water in that river was so dirty, I got a bad infection and had a high temperature for two days.

When you think about it, it was really like a miracle that we all survived this thing. My Mom says that I must have had an angel helping me there, giving me all that strength, and making everything go so well. Maybe she's right, but all I know is that I couldn't have lived if I hadn't saved my mother from that car.

Ask Yourself
Do you think Joseph is a hero? Why or why not?

The Rescue

After the Rescue

A READING *Assessing Strategies*

1. Return to the questions on page 6. Share the answers you found with a partner.
2. Take notes during your discussion and share two points with your class.
3. **a.** Did the questions help you find out what happened to Joseph?

_____

b. Did the headings for each section help you understand the text? Explain.

_____

EXTENDING: Read over your answers on page 6. Add **one** sentence to the chart explaining how Joseph became a hero. Include information about where and how it happened.

B UNDERSTANDING THE SELECTION *Identifying Main Events*

1. Reread each section in the true account. In the **flowchart** below, identify the main event in that section. Use the sequence diagram on pages 8 and 9 to help you.

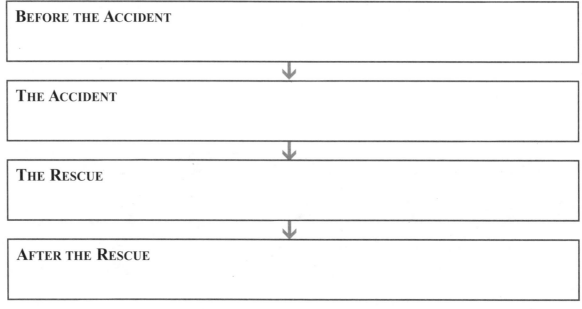

BEFORE THE ACCIDENT

THE ACCIDENT

THE RESCUE

AFTER THE RESCUE

2. **a.** Which do you find easier to understand: the flowchart or the sequence diagram?

_____

b. How has each helped you better understand the true account?

_____

c. As you read "How to Save Someone Who Is Hanging From a Cliff" on page 14, try one of these methods to help you understand the text. Use a flowchart or sequence diagram to identify the steps in the how-to article.

© Gage Learning Corporation

CRITICAL THINKING *Drawing Conclusions*

Use complete sentences to answer the following questions.

1. In your opinion, how was Joseph able to find the courage to rescue his mother and cousin?

_____

_____

2. a. Do you think Joseph thought about the danger to himself during the rescue? _____

b. Give a reason for your answer. _____

_____

_____

3. Describe the bravest thing you have ever done. Were you concerned for your safety?

_____

_____

_____

_____

D VOCABULARY *Understanding Idioms*

- An idiom is an expression that has a meaning different from the dictionary definitions of the individual words in the expression.

    EXAMPLE: Joe and his mother **broke surface**
             MEANS Joe and his mother "came up through the surface of the water."

Place a check mark beside the correct meaning for the <u>underlined</u> idiom in each sentence.

1. Joseph's mother was <u>completely out of it</u> during the rescue.
    ___ totally out of the car   ___ in a risky situation   ___ didn't know what was happening

2. Suddenly <u>it dawned on</u> Joseph that Billy was in the car.
    ___ he remembered Billy   ___ he saw the sun rising   ___ he saw Billy

3. Joseph was <u>losing blood fast</u>.
    ___ noticed his bleeding   ___ was bleeding a lot   ___ didn't know where his blood was

4. Sometimes the Bronco would <u>rev up and then cut down</u>.
    ___ go fast, then slowly   ___ be hard to steer   ___ go up a hill and down the other side

1. Examine the sequence diagram on pages 8 and 9. The Rescue panel of the diagram could be broken into three steps or events. List those steps here.

_____

_____

_____

2. Draw those steps in the panels below.

3. Compare your work with that of a partner. Did you choose the same three steps in the rescue? Explain why your choices are the same or different.

_____

_____

_____

4. Imagine that you've just rescued someone. The rescue scene could be a burning building, a car accident, a near drowning at a local pool, or anything else you can think of.

5. Draw a sequence diagram to show the steps in your heroic rescue. If you need more space, use another piece of paper.

Before Reading
"How to Save Someone Who Is Hanging From a Cliff"

1. What was the most amazing rescue you ever saw in a movie? Describe the rescue to a partner.
2. You're about to read a how-to article about saving someone hanging from a cliff.
    Write down **four** questions you want to find answers to as you read.

a. _____

_____

b. _____

_____

c. _____

_____

d. _____

_____

Asking Questions

Asking questions is a good strategy to use before you begin reading for information. Your questions will help you focus on what you are reading and why you are reading it.

*   **Before reading**, ask questions about what you hope to find out. Write down your questions.
*   **During reading**, think about finding the answers to your questions. Look at your questions from time to time. Write down your answers in point form.
*   **After reading**, check your list to see whether you have found the answers to all your questions.

Further Reading

If you like this selection, you can read similar texts in *The Action Hero's Handbook: How to Catch a Great White Shark, Perform the Vulcan Nerve Pinch, Track a Fugitive, and Dozens of Other TV and Movie Skills* by David and Joe Borgenicht.

How to Save Someone Who Is
HANGING FROM A CLIFF

HOW-TO ARTICLE from *The Action Hero's Handbook* by David Borgenicht and Joe Borgenicht

Warning: The skills taught here are meant for the use of true action heroes only, not for evil geniuses, criminal masterminds, or bad guys of any type. Hey kids, don't try this at home!

> **VOCABULARY**
>
> **anchored**: firmly attached

The expert action hero knows how to save someone hanging by a finger from the edge of a cliff. You must move quickly: unless the victim is <u>anchored</u> to secure ground, you have only a few minutes to pull him or her to safety. If you don't succeed, you may find you have let a close personal friend and climbing partner down (way down).

IF THE VICTIM IS WITHIN YOUR REACH

Step 1: Find solid footing near the victim.
Stand on a surface that you are sure **will not** move: a large rock, a firm ledge, or a live tree. If you are not safe, you may both wind up at the bottom of the cliff.

Step 2: Help the victim stay calm.
The person hanging must stay calm to save as much energy as possible. Also, the victim needs to hold very still, which won't happen if he or she is panicking. No matter how you are able to help the victim, you will need his or her strength to assist you.

> **GOALS AT A GLANCE**
>
> locating information • thinking about action movies

Step 3: Dry your hands.
Use some dry dirt or just wipe your hands on your pants. This is no time for clammy hands.

Step 4: If you have solid footing, use both hands to clasp at least one of the victim's hands.
Otherwise, hold on to a tree or rock with one hand and clasp the victim's hand with the other.

Step 5: If you cannot reach the victim's hand, grab anything he or she is wearing.
If you are looking at a life-or-death situation, just grab anything you can get a solid grip on: a coat, a harness, even hair if it's long enough. There's no time to choose what to grab. But be careful when grabbing clothes; they may be loose and slip off or tear.

Step 6: Pull the victim to safety.
Pulling up an 80-kg person takes serious strength. However, in such a dangerous situation you will likely have a solid dose of <u>adrenalin</u> pumping through your veins to help you. If possible, have the victim climb as you pull.

VOCABULARY

adrenalin: a substance made in the body that gives people in dangerous situations extra energy and strength

15

A   UNDERSTANDING THE SELECTION *Organizing Information*

1. List **four** important things you've learned about how to rescue someone hanging from a cliff. Be sure to explain why each point is important.

Important Point	Why It Is Important

2. The how-to article actually has **six** main points. Explain why you chose the **four** points you did.

_____

_____

_____

EXTENDING: Draw a picture for each step you've listed.

B   CRITICAL THINKING *Personal Connections*

1. Describe what you would do if your best friend fell off a cliff and was hanging from a tree root. Use information from the text.

_____

_____

2. Describe what you would do if your friend were hanging just out of your reach.

_____

_____

3. What would you do if you fell off a cliff and there was no one around to rescue you?

_____

_____

1. With a small group, discuss action movies you have seen. List at least **four** titles here:

_____

_____

2. Examine the Action Movie Web below. Discuss each feature. Now, add at least **two** movie titles for each feature. You can list a movie title more than once.

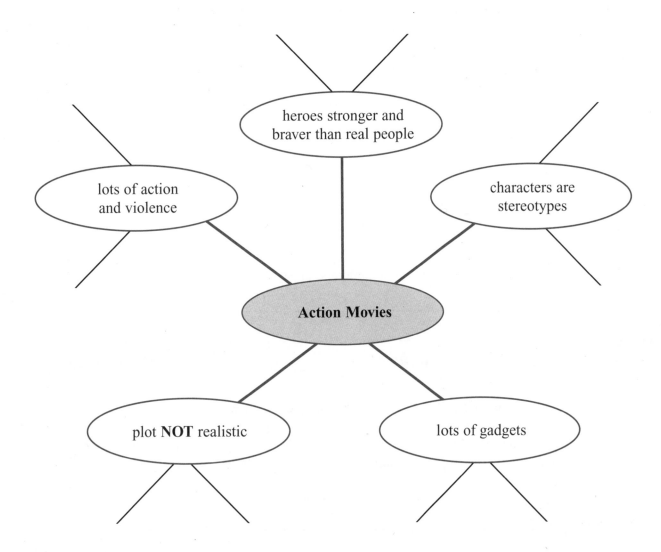

- When you read a new word, you can often figure out its meaning by looking at the words or sentences around it. This is called its **context**.
- Sometimes the meaning or definition of the word is given right in the sentence.
    EXAMPLE: The **expert** action hero <u>knows how</u> to save someone.

- You may find a **synonym** (another word that means the same thing) in the sentence.
    EXAMPLE: Make sure you are <u>attached</u> or **anchored** to a secure object.

- You might find that the opposite of the word is given in the sentence.
    EXAMPLE: Stay **calm**; <u>panic</u> is not an option.

Read each sentence below. Highlight the words that help you figure out the meaning of the <u>underlined</u> word. Write the meaning of the <u>underlined</u> word in the space provided.

1. Find solid <u>footing</u> near the victim and stand on a surface that will not budge.

   _____

2. Just grab anything you can get a solid <u>grip</u> on.

   _____

3. Wipe your hands on your pants, because this is no time for <u>clammy</u> hands.

   _____

4. Hold on to a tree or rock with one hand and <u>clasp</u> his or her hand with the other.

   _____

 E **WRITING** *How-To Article*

1. Write a how-to article about another type of rescue (for example: a car crash, a fire, or an earthquake).
2. Use the selection "How to Save Someone Who Is Hanging From a Cliff" as a model.
3. Write at least **three** steps to explain what the rescuer should do. Tell why each step is necessary.
4. Draw a picture or diagram to go with your how-to article.

TIPS

How-To Article

- Give the information in short, clear steps.
- Arrange the steps in the order they should be done.
- Explain why the steps should be done in the way you are describing them.

Before Reading

Picture this scene: A plane is struck by lightning over the jungle of Peru. The engines catch on fire. The plane breaks apart, scattering victims and wreckage. Can anyone survive this disaster? Read the true story of one passenger.

Against the Jungle

TRUE ACCOUNT by Steve Lawton

❶ It's December 24, 1971. Juliane Koepcke and her mother board a plane to fly from Lima, Peru to Pucallpa, Peru. They're joining Juliane's father in the jungle where he works.

❷ There are 92 people on the plane.

❸ It begins to rain. The plane is tossed about.

❹ Suitcases fall, hitting passengers.

❺ This is the end!

GOALS AT A GLANCE

retelling the story • writing a message

❻ The plane is hit by lightning. It jerks and jolts and breaks up.

❽ In the blink of an eye, Juliane is alone and falling, with no plane around her!

❾ Juliane struggles to breathe as she spins through the air. The jungle gets closer and closer, and she passes out.

❿ Juliane wakes. There is no trace of her mother, other passengers, or crew.

⓫ Juliane has a broken collarbone, swollen eye, and cut foot. She's in shock and does not feel any pain.

⑫ Juliane has only candies to eat and rainwater to drink. She plans to follow the jungle streams to a large river, and then follow the river downstream looking for people.

What am I going to do?

⑬ Juliane sees many wild animals and is afraid this means no people are close. Insects bite Juliane and leave their eggs under her skin.

I hate bugs!

⑭ Juliane is far from any humans or hospital, and her arm is swollen with insect larvae. She is afraid she will lose her arm. She bends her spiral ring into a sharp point to dig out the maggots.

⑮ Juliane has no candies left and does not know how much longer she'll be in the jungle. Finally, she comes to a large river with a strong current.

Don't give up! Just jump in and swim!

⑯ Juliane's arm is not healing. She knows she must get help soon or she will lose her arm. She is hungry, hurt, tired, and worried. She knows she must keep going.

⑰ Juliane rests. She hears voices and turns to see two men. She has been in the jungle for ten days. She has walked out, despite her injuries, her hunger, her loss. She is the only survivor.

A   UNDERSTANDING THE SELECTION *Retelling the Story*

1. Return to the text and circle **five** important details in Juliane's story.
2. Imagine you are Juliane telling a friend what happened to you. Tell a partner about the plane crash and your time in the jungle. Include in your retelling the **five** details you circled.
3. Explain to your partner how retelling the story helped you understand it better. Would you use this strategy again? Why or why not?

B   CRITICAL THINKING *Drawing Conclusions*

1. Why did Juliane not feel her injuries at first? _____

   _____

2. Why did Juliane follow the river? _____

   _____

3. **a.** What was Juliane afraid of as she walked through the jungle? _____

   _____

   b. What would you be afraid of in the same situation? _____

   _____

4. What helped Juliane survive? _____

   _____

5. What part of Juliane's story did you find the most interesting? Why? _____

   _____

Drawing Conclusions

- To answer a question that asks you to draw a logical conclusion, first think about what the selection **does** tell you about the topic.
- Then, search for other clues in the selection that will help you draw a logical conclusion or make an educated guess.
- Make connections between the facts and ideas in the selection and your own experiences and understanding.
- Check that your answer makes sense, given what you know from the selection.

WRITING *Message in a Bottle*

1. Imagine that Juliane had a pencil, notepad, and juice bottle. She reached the river and decided to send a message in a bottle. She hoped that someone would find it and help her.
2. Write the message she might have sent. Include dates and names of places from the article.

To Whom It May Concern:

My name is Juliane Koepcke and _____

_____

_____

_____

_____

_____

_____ .

3. Read over your message. Check that it contains enough information that a reader would be

    able to help Juliane. What would you add? _____

    _____

VOCABULARY *Words About Heroes*

1. What words do you think of when you hear the word **hero**? Add those words to the following word web.

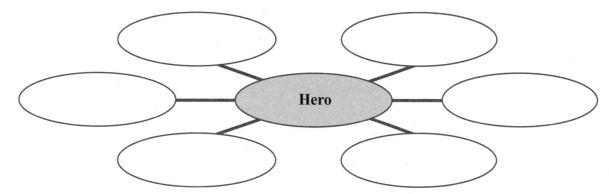

2. Compare your word web with that of a partner.
3. What words from your word web would you use to describe Juliane?

- Use a **period** (.) at the end of a statement. A **statement** is a sentence that tells you something.
  - EXAMPLE: The engines catch on fire.

- Use a **period** at the end of a command. A **command** is a sentence that orders you to do something
  - EXAMPLE: Don't give up.

- Use a **question mark** (?) at the end of a question. A **question** is a sentence that asks something.
  - EXAMPLE: Can anyone survive this disaster?

- Use an **exclamation mark** at the end of an exclamation. An **exclamation** is a sentence that shows strong feeling.
  - EXAMPLE: This is the end!

Use the correct punctuation mark at the end of each sentence below. Write the kind of sentence it is: **statement**, **command**, **question**, or **exclamation**.

1. Do you believe this story _____

2. It's December 24, 1971 _____

3. I **hate** mosquitoes _____

4. Why did the plane crash _____

5. Juliane fell through the air _____

6. Hand me that suitcase _____

7. How did Juliane survive _____

8. Help _____

9. Follow the river downstream _____

Using End Punctuation

- Using the correct end punctuation makes your writing easier to understand.
- After you finish a piece of writing, read it aloud to check that you have used the correct end punctuation.
- If you say a sentence with strong feeling, it probably needs an exclamation mark. If your voice goes up at the end of a sentence, it probably needs a question mark.

UNIT 1 WRAP-UP

SELF-ASSESSMENT *Reading Strategies*

1. Choose **one** point below. In your notebook, explain what you learned about this reading strategy.

   ❏ drawing a diagram to show the sequence of events in a text
   ❏ asking questions before and during reading
   ❏ working out the meaning of a word by looking at its context
   ❏ drawing conclusions about what you have read

2. Think about the selections you have read in this unit. In your notebook, describe at least **two** reading strategies that helped you read or understand the selections.

3. Set a goal for improving your use of **one** of the above reading strategies. Explain what you will do.

_____

_____

PROJECT IDEA *Real Heroes*

Create a small book to honour someone you know who is a <u>real hero</u>. It might be a family member, friend, teacher, or someone else in your community.

Step 1. Think about the person you want to honour. In your notebook, write at least four sentences to describe that person.

Step 2. Use your description to write a statement about who your hero is and what makes this person a hero. Write this statement in your notebook.

> My definition of a real hero is (insert name here) because \\\\\\\\\\\\\\
> \\\\\\\\\\\\\\\\\\\\\
> \\\\\\\\\\\\\\\\\\\\\\
> \\\\\\\\\\\\\\\\\\\\\

Step 3. Ask your hero to say something about what it's like to be a hero. That can become your quotation. Use the quotations on page 3 as a model.

Step 4. Write instructions (with the help of your hero) to explain something the hero does every day. Use the how-to article on page 7 as a model.

Step 5. Ask your hero to tell you about a time when he or she was a real hero. Create drawings to show what your hero did. Use the sequence diagram on page 8 or the true account on page 19 as a model.

Step 6. On at least **five** blank pieces of paper, organize all of the work you have produced. Create a good title for your book. Create a cover with a drawing or photo of your hero.

The strategy of asking questions helps you to better understand what you are reading. Asking questions also helps you keep your mind focused on what you are reading. You can use this strategy before, during, or after reading a selection.

BEFORE READING

Ask yourself questions about the title and subject of the selection. Good questions include:

- What is this selection going to be about?
- What do I already know about this subject?
- What do I want to find out?

DURING READING

Ask yourself questions as you read. Think about your experiences and knowledge. Good question starters include:

- What did the author mean when he/she said...?
- If this is true, does that mean...?
- What examples of this can I think of from my own life?

AFTER READING

Think about what you have just read. Form some new questions. Good question starters include:

- What if...?
- I wonder what...?
- Why is it important for me to know this?
- Who else should know this?

SETTING GOALS

The next time you read a text in this book, write down at least **two** questions before, during, and after reading. Afterward, think about how these questions helped increase your understanding of the text.

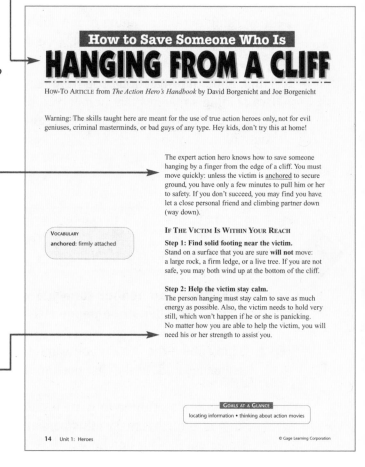

How to Save Someone Who Is
HANGING FROM A CLIFF

How-To Article from *The Action Hero's Handbook* by David Borgenicht and Joe Borgenicht

Warning: The skills taught here are meant for the use of true action heroes only, not for evil geniuses, criminal masterminds, or bad guys of any type. Hey kids, don't try this at home!

The expert action hero knows how to save someone hanging by a finger from the edge of a cliff. You must move quickly: unless the victim is anchored to secure ground, you have only a few minutes to pull him or her to safety. If you don't succeed, you may find you have let a close personal friend and climbing partner down (way down).

VOCABULARY
anchored: firmly attached

IF THE VICTIM IS WITHIN YOUR REACH

Step 1: Find solid footing near the victim.
Stand on a surface that you are sure **will not** move: a large rock, a firm ledge, or a live tree. If you are not safe, you may both wind up at the bottom of the cliff.

Step 2: Help the victim stay calm.
The person hanging must stay calm to save as much energy as possible. Also, the victim needs to hold very still, which won't happen if he or she is panicking. No matter how you are able to help the victim, you will need his or her strength to assist you.

GOALS AT A GLANCE
locating information • thinking about action movies

14   Unit 1: Heroes   © Gage Learning Corporation

Before Reading
"The Way of a Winner"

Think about your family and friends. What lessons about life have they taught you? What is the **most** important thing you have learned from someone close to you? Discuss your answers with a partner. Write down your thoughts on these questions.

_____

_____

_____

_____

During Reading

The following **memoir** was written by a teenager, Jessie Bruneau, for a contest about Aboriginal heroes. Jesse writes about his father. As you read, record **five** details about the father's physical appearance and **five** details about his personality.

memoir: a record of a person's experiences, like a diary or journal.

Father's Physical Appearance	Father's Personality

The Way of a Winner

MEMOIR by Jesse Marcel Bruneau

Ever since I was a small boy I'd looked up to my dad, but the summer I was ten he became a hero for real. That was the year he won his first canoe championship.

He was six foot two [188 cm] and close to 200 pounds [91 kg]. He was tall, strong, and good-looking and pulled his pickup truck around the driveway just for the exercise. He could run faster, jump higher, and hit harder than anybody around, but he'd never been in a canoe in his life before deciding he was going to win that race. It was put on by a local reserve and two weeks later the town of Cold Lake had one. He decided he'd win that one too.

He was hard-headed that way. If he got an idea in his head you couldn't shake it loose. Sometimes that was good. He used to say that he was "the greatest" but we knew he had reason to be confident in his strength.

He'd never lost a fight. His other side was funny and gentle and affectionate. He loved to play and he loved Mom and me. He liked living quietly and was leaving his rowdy days behind. But he was like an old gunfighter who wanted to hang up his guns but somebody always wanted to try him out and take him on. They always regretted it.

VOCABULARY

voyageur: a person who worked for early fur-trading companies, travelling by canoe and trapping animals

North West Company: refers to the North West Trading Company, a group of fur-trading companies

endurance: the power to last or keep on

GOALS AT A GLANCE

recalling information • reading between the lines

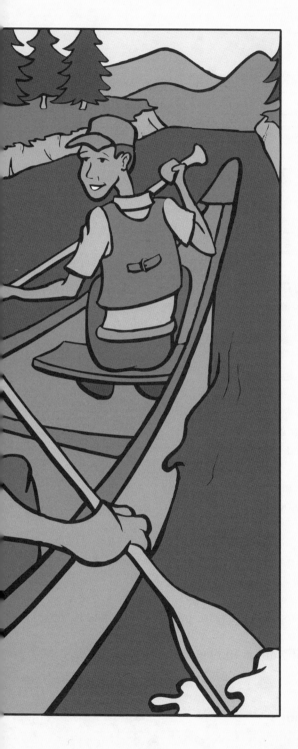

I don't know where he got the canoeing idea, maybe it was after Mom traced his ancestry back to a <u>voyageur</u> who worked for the <u>North West Company</u> in the 1700s. Wherever he got it from, he decided he was going to win that trophy. After he decided that, he got mad at people who tried to discourage him.

He believed in himself and dropped the people who didn't. He picked his partner, Wesley Deep, and then he was set. Together for the first time they made one practice run and the next day paddled flat out for seven miles [over 11 km] and won the race. The other canoes weren't even in sight when Dad and Wes hit the beach. All their races were like that. Dad never once questioned his ability to win and that God would help him. He never gave up.

* * * * *

As he went on to win eight more trophies in four years, my outlook on life changed. After he died in November 1991, I realized I'd had a good role model who taught me, by example, a formula for success in life.

Probably the first thing I learned is that having a hard life, a poor and violent childhood like he'd had, only got you down if you let it. He used his to toughen himself up. He showed me that championships come from the head and the heart, not the background.

Because he believed in himself against all odds, I learned that nothing was impossible if I set my mind to it. I learned to believe that the thing I wanted would come to me and to fight for it if I had to. I learned never to allow myself to get discouraged or doubt I'd reach my goal.

The most important thing I learned was that faith, <u>endurance</u>, and patience would help me overcome any challenge in life.

Complete this "i" chart for
"The Way of a Winner." You can
use point form.

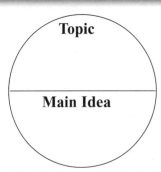

Topic

Main Idea

Details (list **three**)

_____

_____

_____

B   UNDERSTANDING THE SELECTION *Recalling Information*

1. This memoir takes place
   a. in recent times   **b.** in the 1700s
   c. in the future   **d.** in someone's imagination

2. Jesse's father decided to try canoe racing after
   a. he won his first race   **b.** he was challenged to race
   c. his truck broke down   **d.** his wife traced his ancestry

3. After Jesse's father died, Jesse realized that his father had been
   a. good at winning   **b.** a good role model
   c. a good fighter   **d.** sad

4. What is the best meaning for the word **hard-headed** in the third paragraph on page 28?
   a. stubborn   **b.** indestructible   **c.** sensible   **d.** painless

5. What is the best meaning for the word **outlook** as it is used in the third paragraph on page 29?
   a. place to get a good view   **b.** a lookout
   c. way to look at the future   **d.** way of thinking about things

Answering Multiple-Choice Questions
- Read each question or statement carefully.
- Cross out those answers that you immediately identify as wrong.
- Skim the selection for key words used in the question or answers.
- Check that your answer makes sense.

C CRITICAL THINKING *Reading Between the Lines*

1. Why do you think Jesse's dad was so determined to win the race? Use the text to explain your answer.

_____

_____

2. What do you think was the most important lesson Jesse learned from his dad?

_____

_____

3. Describe Jesse Bruneau. Because Jesse does not describe himself, you will need to "read between the lines" to answer this question.

_____

_____

4. Reread the last **four** paragraphs of the text. If his father had not died when Jesse was 14, do you think Jesse's outlook would still have changed? Support your answer using the text.

_____

_____

Reading Between the Lines

When you are reading, you often need to figure out the meaning **behind** what the writer is saying.
- Ask yourself: "Why did the writer tell me that? What does the writer mean here?"
- Think about the clues that the writer is giving about events and characters.

D WRITING *Personal Response*

1. In your notebook, write at least **one** paragraph about "The Way of a Winner." Use the following questions as a starting point:
   - How does "The Way of a Winner" make you feel?
   - What ideas or thoughts about the memoir did you have as you read?
   - What events or people in your own life does this memoir remind you of? Explain why.

2. Responding personally to a text can help you understand and enjoy it. In your notebook, explain how writing a personal response to this text changed your thoughts about it.

Before Reading
"O Siem"

Look over the song and photo on the next page. Answer the following questions.

1. What do you think about when you read the title of the song?

    _____

    _____

2. **a.** What do you notice about how the song looks (the length or number of lines, language, and so on)?

    _____

    _____

    b. What other kind of writing does the song look like?

    _____

    _____

3. What does the photo suggest the song will be about?

    _____

    _____

Reading Strategies

Previewing a Text
- Looking over a text helps to prepare you for reading it.
- Note any special features such as pictures, photos, headings, charts, or boxes.
- Notice whether parts of the text are in **bold face** type.
- Think about how the text is similar to material you have read in the past. Think about similar reading strategies you could use for this new text.

VOCABULARY

Chorus: part of a song that is repeated

O Siem: an exclamation of joy at seeing friends and family

Siem o siyeya: all peoples, all cultures and races, all people rich and poor

O Siem

SONG by Susan Aglukark and Chad Irschick

<u>**Chorus:**</u>
<u>O siem</u>
We are all family
O siem
We're all the same
O siem
The fires of freedom
Dance in the burning flame.

<u>Siem o siyeya</u>
All people rich and poor
Siem o siyeya
Those who do and do not know
Siem o siyeya
Take the hand of one close by
Siem o siyeya
Of those who know because they try
And watch the walls come tumbling down.

Repeat chorus

Siem o siyeya
All people of the world
Siem o siyeya
It's time to make the turn
Siem o siyeya
A chance to share your heart
Siem o siyeya
To make a brand new start
And watch the walls come tumbling down.

Repeat chorus

Susan Aglukark is an Inuk singer; she has included two phrases from her native language in this song.

GOALS AT A GLANCE

personal response • making inferences

UNDERSTANDING THE SELECTION *Personal Response*

Use complete sentences to answer the following.

1. a. How did the song make you feel? _____

_____

b. Why did you feel that way? _____

_____

_____

2. a. What part of this song did you like best? _____

_____

b. What did you like about that part? _____

_____

CRITICAL THINKING *Making Inferences*

In songs and poetry, writers often use language that means more than it says. For example, We are all family means that "all people in the world are related or connected to one another."

1. Find each of these phrases in the song. Explain what they mean in your own words.

a. We're all the same _____

b. It's time to make the turn _____

c. share your heart _____

d. watch the walls come tumbling down _____

2. Select **one** phrase from question B1 and explain how it helps communicate the message of the song.

_____

_____

EXTENDING: With a partner, discuss the following questions:
- What might have been Susan Aglukark's reason for writing this song?
- Give one possible reason why Susan included words from her native language in this song.

Take notes during your discussion. Share **two** points from the discussion with the class.

VISUAL COMMUNICATION *Drawing an Illustration*

1. Reread the song. What pictures do you see in your mind? Choose **one** picture and describe it.

   _____

   _____

2. Use your description to draw an illustration for "O Siem."
3. Share your illustration with a classmate. Discuss it.

> **TIPS**
>
> **Illustrating**
>
> Illustrations can help explain written material.
> • Choose an idea, location, or event from the text.
> • Decide on the materials you wish to use for your illustration, for example, pencil, marker, pencil crayons, or paint.
> • Make some sketches testing out your ideas.
> • Make a good copy of your illustration when you are ready.

D

WRITING *Opinions*

Complete the following statements about music.

1. My favourite kind of music is _____.

2. I like it because _____.

3. My favourite recording artist/group is _____.

4. I like him/her/them because _____.

5. Some people don't like my music because they think _____.

6. I disagree with these people because _____.

EXTENDING: Use the ideas above to write an opinion paragraph about your favourite kind of music.

   _____

   _____

   _____

   _____

> • **Homophones** are words that sound alike but have different meanings and spellings.
>   EXAMPLES: it's, its
>   one, won
>   your, you're
>   know, no

1. Complete each sentence by choosing the correct homophone in the brackets.

   a. _____ time to make the turn. (It's, Its)

   b. When the wall tumbled, _____ stones landed on my foot. (it's, its)

   c. We have _____ our fight for peace. (one, won)

   d. Take the hand of _____ close by. (one, won)

   e. _____ always helping others (Your, You're)

   f. It's a chance to share _____ heart. (your, you're)

   g. They _____ because they try. (know, no)

   h. There's _____ use denying we're all family. (know, no)

2. Write sentences for **four** of the homophones above, showing their correct meaning.

   _____

   _____

   _____

   _____

   _____

   _____

Homophones
• After you have used a homophone in your writing, read the sentence over again.
• Check that you have the right homophone. One way to do that is to switch the homophone with its meaning to see if it makes sense. For example, try **it's**, meaning <u>it is</u> or **its**, meaning <u>belonging to it</u>.

   CORRECT: The dog lost <u>its</u> (belonging to it) ball.

   INCORRECT: The dog lost <u>it's</u> (it is) ball.

Before Reading

Severn Cullis-Suzuki is very concerned about the environment. As a young Canadian student, she spoke out about her concerns to a large audience of people from around the world. They were all in Rio de Janeiro, Brazil to discuss global environmental problems.

TELL THE WORLD

SPEECH by Severn Cullis-Suzuki

Hello, I'm Severn Cullis-Suzuki speaking on behalf of ECO, the Environmental Children's Organization. We're a group of 12- and 13-year-olds from Canada trying to make a difference.

We raised all the money ourselves to come 6000 miles [over 9600 km] to tell you adults you **must** change your ways.

I am here to speak for all future generations. I am here to speak on behalf of the starving children around the world whose cries go unheard. I am here to speak for the countless animals dying across this planet because they have nowhere left to go.

I am afraid to go out in the sun now because of the holes in the ozone. I am afraid to breathe the air because I don't know what chemicals are in it. I used to go fishing in Vancouver with my dad, until just a few years ago we found the fish full of cancers. And now we hear about animals and plants becoming extinct every day, vanishing forever.

In my life, I have dreamt of seeing great herds of wild animals, jungles, and rain forests full of birds and butterflies, but now I wonder if they will even exist for my children to see. Did you have to worry about these things when you were my age?

GOALS AT A GLANCE

organizing information • using commas

VOCABULARY

delegates: people who represent others, speaking up for their interests and rights

All this is happening before our eyes and yet we act as if we have all the time we want and all the solutions. I'm only a child and I don't have all the solutions, but I want you to realize, neither do you!

You don't know how to fix the holes in our ozone layer. You don't know how to bring salmon back to a dead stream. You don't know how to bring back an animal now extinct. And you can't bring back the forests that once grew where there is now a desert. If you don't know how to fix it, please stop breaking it!

Here you may be <u>delegates</u> of your governments, business people, organizers, reporters, or politicians. But really, you are mothers and fathers, sisters and brothers, aunts and uncles. And each of you is somebody's child.

I'm only a child, yet I know we are all part of a family, five-billion strong, in fact, 30-million species strong, and borders and governments will never change that. I'm only a child, yet I know we are all in this together and should act as one single world toward one single goal. In my anger I am not blind, and in my fear I'm not afraid to tell the world how I feel.

In my country we make so much waste. We buy and throw away, buy and throw away. And yet northern countries will not share with the needy. Even when we have more than enough, we are afraid to lose some of our wealth, afraid to let go.

In Canada, we live a privileged life with plenty of food, water, and shelter. We have watches, bicycles, computers, and television sets; the list could go on for days.

By Evangelina Maya, age 18

Two days ago here in Brazil, we were shocked when we spent time with some children living on the streets. And this is what one child told us: "I wish I was rich. And if I were, I would give all the street children food, clothes, medicine, shelter, and love and affection." If a child on the street who has nothing is willing to share, why are we who have everything still so greedy?

I can't stop thinking that these children are my own age, and that it makes a tremendous difference where you are born. I could be one of those children living in the **favellas** (slums) of Rio, I could be a child starving in Somalia, a victim of war in the Middle East, or a beggar in India.

I'm only a child, yet I know if all the money spent on **war** was spent on ending poverty and finding environmental answers, what a wonderful place this Earth would be.

Thank you for listening.

By Esther Choi, age 15

1. When she gave this speech, Severn was
   a. a student from Brazil
   b. a famous scientist
   c. a well-known speech writer
   d. a Canadian student

2. What was Severn's personal experience with water pollution?

   _____

   _____

   _____

3. Severn thinks that adults should listen to children about these issues because

   _____

   _____

   _____

4. How do the drawings support the ideas in the speech? Refer to at least **one** drawing in your answer.

   _____

   _____

   _____

B VISUAL COMMUNICATION *Collage*

Choose one idea from this selection that you feel strongly about. Follow these steps to create a <u>collage</u> for this idea.

1. Find photos or drawings that represent that idea. You might also want to create drawings.
2. Find headlines, slogans, or other pieces of text that express your idea.
3. Cut up your materials and arrange them on a piece of paper. Try out different arrangements until you find one you like. Paste your materials to the page.
4. Give your collage a title.

A **collage** is a picture made by arranging items with different textures, colours, and shapes on a background. You can use both visual and print texts to create your collage.

CRITICAL THINKING *Organizing Information*

1. In her speech, Severn talks about three kinds of problems: environmental, animal, and human. For each statement below, label the kind of problem being described. <u>Underline</u> the key words that helped you decide.

_____ **a.** I am here to speak on behalf of the starving children around the world whose cries go unheard.

_____ **b.** I am here to speak for the countless animals dying across this planet because they have nowhere left to go.

_____ **c.** I am afraid to breathe the air because I don't know what chemicals are in it.

_____ **d.** I used to go fishing in Vancouver with my dad, until just a few years ago we found the fish full of cancers.

_____ **e.** You don't know how to bring back an animal now extinct.

_____ **f.** We buy and throw away, buy and throw away.

2. Use the **letters** (a to f) to organize all of the above statements into the correct column in the chart below.

Environmental	Animal	Human

3. Look at the chart and then look at each statement again. Is there any statement that could be given more than one label? Explain.

_____

_____

D WRITER'S CRAFT *A Speech*

Writers use **speeches** to share their ideas with an audience. They often use the following **techniques** to make a speech more effective:

• Writers may use **repetition** of words and phrases to catch the attention of listeners.
>   EXAMPLE: <u>I am here to speak</u> for all future generations. <u>I am here to speak</u>
>   on behalf of the starving children around the world....

• Writers often use **questions** to connect with the audience.
>   EXAMPLE: Did you have to worry about these things when you were my age?

• **Emotional words** help writers to convince their audience to share their ideas.
>   EXAMPLE: I am here to speak for the <u>countless animals dying</u> across this planet.

1. Find **one** more example of each of these techniques in "Tell the World." <u>Underline</u> and label each example: **repetition**, **question**, or **emotional words**.

2. Do you think that Severn's speech is effective? Give a reason for your answer.

_____

_____

E LANGUAGE CONVENTIONS *Commas*

• A **comma (,)** shows a slight pause in a sentence. Commas help you to understand the writer's meaning.
>   EXAMPLE: Hello, I'm Severn Suzuki speaking on behalf of ECO,
>   the Environmental Children's Organization.

• Use commas between words or groups of words in a series. Use **and** before the last item.
>   EXAMPLE: Suzuki spoke about the extinction of birds, insects, and plants.

Add commas where needed in the following sentences. The number of commas needed is shown in brackets.

1. Speaking today the delegate from Brazil asked us to help clean up the oceans. (1)

2. Scientists politicians and environmentalists came to the conference. (2)

3. Finally we understand the danger of careless habits. (1)

4. Pop cans food wrappers and plastic bags littered the beach. (2)

5. Suddenly everyone we know is thinking about the environment. (1)

6. There are many kinds of reptiles birds mammals and insects. (3)

7. Our school has formed its own organization Friends of the World. (1)

WHOEVER SAID DON'T RUN...

POSTCARD from Kids Help Phone

WHOEVER SAID DON'T RUN FROM YOUR PROBLEMS NEVER HAD TO FACE A BULLY.

KIDS HELP PHONE
1 800 668 6868

THERE'S A LOT ON THE LINE.

Front of postcard.

The organization Kids Help Phone gives out postcards with information about common problems faced by young people. This is one of their cards.

GOALS AT A GLANCE

responding to an image • summarizing

KIDS HELP PHONE
What To Do About Bullying

Bullying is scary and embarrassing. It can make you feel as if it's your fault. It's not!

There are things you can do to make bullies stop. Here are some **tips**:

1. Stay calm and don't act upset or angry: bullies love to get a <u>reaction</u>. Practise what you'll do and say the next time it happens. If you don't act upset or react the way they want you to, they might get bored and stop.

2. Don't fight back. If you fight back, you could make the situation worse, get hurt, or be blamed for starting the trouble.

3. Try to calmly <u>withdraw</u> from the situation. Try to ignore the bullying or say "no" really firmly, then turn and walk away calmly. It's very hard for the bully to go on bullying someone who won't stand still to listen.

4. If it's either you or your stuff, give up your stuff. Things can be replaced. You can't.

5. Avoid being alone in places where you know the bully is likely to pick on you. It's not fair that you have to do this but it might put the bully off until you talk to an adult or find another solution to stop the bullying.

6. Avoid being alone as much as you can. Whenever possible, travel with others to and from school and to special school events. Stick with a group, even if they are not your friends.

7. Don't be afraid to tell an adult you trust, like a teacher or your mom or dad. You don't have to let them take over. You can talk with them about what you would like to happen.

Most of all, don't give up. Being bullied can make you feel really bad about yourself and very discouraged. This is exactly what the bullies are hoping for. If you give in, they will be able to take advantage of you in different ways and at different times. If you are feeling like giving up, make sure you talk to someone. Don't forget **Kids Help Phone at 1-800-668-6868** is always <u>confidential</u> and free.

Back of postcard.

1. What is the message of the photo and words on the front of the postcard?

_____

2. Who is the intended audience for the card? Why do you think so?

_____

_____

3. What did you notice first: the photo or the words? Why? _____

_____

_____

4. Why do you think this photo was chosen for the card? _____

_____

_____

B CRITICAL THINKING *Summarizing*

In one sentence, summarize the main idea of each tip on page 44. The first one has been done for you.

1. Don't show your emotions and the bully might leave you alone.

2. _____

3. _____

4. _____

5. _____

6. _____

7. _____

Comprehension Strategies

Summarizing

To **summarize** is to make a brief statement giving the main points of a text.
- Read the material over two or three times. <u>Underline</u> or highlight the key phrases.
- In your own words, write a sentence that tells the most important ideas.
- Your summary should be much shorter than the original material.

- A **slogan** is a short, easy-to-remember message.
  EXAMPLE: The Calgary Humane Society: <u>Positively Animal Since 1922</u>

- Advertisers often use slogans to sell products to their audience.
  EXAMPLE: Nike: <u>Just Do It</u>

- Slogans often play with the different meanings of words.
  EXAMPLE: The United Way (a charity): <u>Without you, there would be no way</u>
  The words **no way** mean "<u>no way</u> for the United Way to do its good works."
  No way also means "<u>no</u> United <u>Way</u>."

---

1. "There's a Lot on the Line" is one of the slogans for Kids Help Phone. One meaning for this slogan is "Important things (kids' lives) are at risk." What other meaning for the word **line** might apply to the slogan?

   _____

   _____

2. Kids Help Phone also uses the slogan "Being There for Kids." What does this slogan mean?

   _____

   _____

   _____

3. Which slogan do you think is more effective? Explain why you like it.

   _____

   _____

   _____

   _____

4. Suggest **one** new slogan for Kids Help Phone.

   _____

   _____

EXTENDING: Think of **one** other reason young people might phone Kids Help Phone.
Develop a slogan and design a postcard for that problem. Remember to create both
a front (with photo and slogan) and a back (with tips) for your postcard.

In the speech bubbles below, young people talk about some of their experiences.

1. With three other students, discuss the advice you would give these young people.
2. In the blank bubble beside each speech bubble, write **one** piece of advice.

> My best friend always drops me when someone cool comes along.

Marie, 13

> I often make jokes that hurt my friends, but I can't stop going for cheap laughs.

Sara, 12

> I'm shy, and it's hard for me to make friends.

Vince, 13

> My best friend is in big trouble and I don't know how to help him.

Luigi, 14

3. Think about the way you completed this activity. Write down **one** thing you did really well.

_____

Write down **one** thing you will improve next time.

_____

Group Discussion
- Listen to what others are saying.
- Wait for your turn to speak.
- Stay on topic when you are speaking.
- Respect everyone in the group.

UNIT 2 WRAP-UP

SELF-ASSESSMENT *Visual/Oral Communication Activities*

1. Check off each activity listed below that you completed during this unit:

   ❏ illustrating a song
   ❏ creating a collage
   ❏ analysing a speech
   ❏ responding to an image
   ❏ group discussion about advice

2. Choose **one** of the items you checked above. In your notebook, explain what you did and what you learned from completing the activity.

PROJECT IDEA *A Speech*

In this unit, you read a speech (page 37) and analysed the techniques the writer used to share her ideas effectively with her audience (page 42). Use what you learned to write a speech about a topic raised in this unit.

Step 1. Think about the selections you read in this unit. For each selection, suggest at least **one** topic to give a speech about.

    The Way of a Winner: _____

    O Siem: _____

    Tell the World: _____

    Whoever Said Don't Run... _____

Step 2. Choose **one** topic from your list for your speech.

Step 3. Brainstorm a list of ideas on the topic that you would like to include in your speech. Organize your ideas into an outline.

Step 4. Write your speech, stating your ideas and feelings on the topic. Use the speech-writing techniques on page 42 to help you make your speech effective.

Step 5. Practise your speech. Read it to a partner. Ask for feedback on how you can improve the content and delivery of your speech.

Step 6. Present your speech to a group or to your class.

> **OUTLINE**
>
> **Topic**
> • First Idea
>   ≡ *Support*
>
> • Second Idea
>   ≡ *Support*
>
> • Third Idea
>   ≡ *Support*

Summarizing a text can help you to understand it better. Summarizing is also an important note-taking skill. Here's how to create a summary of a text.

Selection
Reread **all** of the selection. Make sure that you understand what it is about. If you are confused, discuss it with your teacher or a classmate.

Paragraphs or Sections
Focus on **one** paragraph or **one** section of the text at a time. Skim the section and underline the most important words.

Main Ideas
Decide how the words that you underlined are related to one another. What is the main idea of the section?

Here, the author has listed several environmental problems, but the key words are **pollution** and **extinction**.

TELL THE WORLD

I am here to speak for all future generations. I am here to speak on behalf of the starving children around the world whose cries go unheard. I am here to speak for the countless animals dying across this planet because they have nowhere left to go.

I am afraid to go out in the sun now because of the holes in the ozone. I am afraid to breathe the air because I don't know what chemicals are in it. I used to go fishing in Vancouver with my dad, until just a few years ago we found the fish full of cancers. And now we hear about animals and plants becoming extinct every day, vanishing forever.

Summarize in Your Own Words
Use your own words to restate the main ideas of a text. For example, life on Earth is being threatened by pollution is the main idea of the second paragraph.

Setting Goals
How good are you at summarizing texts? How might you improve your use of this skill? Suggest **one** way to improve your summarizing skills over the next month.

_____

_____

Before Reading

How far would you go to be "in" or "cool"? Below, some teenagers describe things they have done to be cool.

Stupid Things I Did to Be COOL

ONLINE ARTICLE from *Zillions® Magazine, Consumer Reports® for Kids*

I SHAVED MY HEAD TO IMPRESS OLDER KIDS

When I was 13, I went out for wrestling. I shaved my head bald so the older wrestlers on the team would think I was cool. It didn't work. They laughed at me and so did kids my age.

Tom, 19

I DITCHED MY OLD FRIENDS TO IMPRESS OTHER KIDS

When I was 14, I thought my old friends weren't cool enough for me. So I ditched them to impress the cool group. It was stupid and didn't make me more popular. I tried to win back my old friends, but it didn't work.

Robbie, 18

> **GOALS AT A GLANCE**
>
> examining reasons • responding personally

I PERMED MY HAIR TO LOOK COOL

Perms were all the rage. So I got my long, thick, beautiful hair <u>transformed</u> into a short, layered, curly bob. It totally backfired on me. I looked like a nine-year-old with 60-year-old hair.

Tara, 17

VOCABULARY

transformed: changed radically

I FILLED MY CLOSET WITH BRAND-NAME CLOTHES

In junior high, I bought only expensive brand-name clothes, "the" clothes to wear. I wanted to impress the popular crowd. It made no difference. The "cool" crowd didn't admit members based on clothes. It was stupid to have spent so much money for nothing.

Sarah, 18

A. UNDERSTANDING THE SELECTION *Examining Reasons*

1. Complete the following chart.

What the Teenagers Did to Show They Were Cool	What Happened?

2. Why was being cool so important to the teenagers in the selection?

_____

_____

3. Think of some other ways people try to show they are cool. List at least **two** ideas.

_____

_____

B. CRITICAL THINKING *Personal Response*

As you answer these questions, think about your own experiences.

1. **a.** Whose story in "Stupid Things I Did to Be Cool" did you like best? _____

   b. Why did you like that story best? _____

   _____

2. How would you define **cool**? _____

   _____

3. Why do you think some people don't worry about being cool? _____

   _____

   _____

Reflecting

4. Did you find questions 1 to 3 easy or difficult to answer? Explain. _____

   _____

   _____

During Reading

While you are reading the following script, think about who is lying and why he is lying. After you have read the script once, circle each lie. In the margin, explain why that person might be lying.

Skate Secrets

<u>SCRIPT</u> from *A Lunch Line* by Carleen Jennings

Ricky:	So you can be on the skateboarding team?
JT:	No problem.
Ricky:	You know how to skate?
JT:	Are you kidding?
Ricky:	You can handle a big skateboard?
JT:	Sure.
Ricky:	What kind of board do you have?
JT:	Uh…umm…what's the best?
Ricky:	Natas.
JT:	That's what I've got.
Ricky:	What's your best move?
JT:	Name some.
Ricky:	Ollie, handplant, rail slide.
JT:	That's it. A rail slide.

> **CHARACTERS:** Ricky, a cool kid
> JT, wants to be cool
>
> **SETTING:** Schoolyard after school

> **GOALS AT A GLANCE**
>
> demonstrating understanding • making inferences

> **VOCABULARY**
>
> **Script**: the written text of a play

Ricky: You can rail slide?

JT: Yup.

Ricky: It took me months to learn that.

JT: It did?

Ricky: I'm still not really good at it. But with an expert like you on our team, we're going to bury those other guys in the dust! Right?

JT: Right.

Ricky: See you Thursday at practice. You know, the guys said you couldn't really skate. I can't wait to see their faces when you rail slide.

(Ricky exits.)

JT: What am I going to do? I can't skate. My Mom won't even let me touch a skateboard. How the heck am I going to rail slide? What **is** a rail slide? I hang around Ricky and the guys because they're cool. Nobody knew my secret. Now I've got three days to learn everything in the world about skateboarding. I'm dead meat!

UNDERSTANDING THE SELECTION *Demonstrating Understanding*

1. **a.** At what point in the script did you realize JT is just pretending to be a skateboarder?

   _____

   b. How did you know? _____

   _____

2. Why does JT lie to Ricky about his skill with a skateboard? _____

   _____

3. Why do you think Ricky asks JT to be on the team? _____

   _____

   EXTENDING: What do you think will happen on Thursday at the practice? Explain your answer.

B

CRITICAL THINKING *Making Inferences*

1. Think about JT's **dialogue** (the words a character speaks). He says very little, but there is probably a lot going on in his head as he tries to give the right answers to Ricky.

   For example, when JT answers "No problem" to Ricky's first question, he might be thinking: "I really want to be on the team so that I can hang around with you guys."

2. Locate the following lines in the script. Write down what JT might be thinking as he speaks.

What JT Says	What JT Is Thinking
Are you kidding?	
That's what I've got.	
Name some.	
It did?	
Right.	

Reflecting

3. Describe the process you went through to complete this activity. _____

   _____

   _____

1. With a partner, write the dialogue for a second **scene** between Ricky and JT. Use "Skate Secrets" as a model.
2. Your scene could take place before or after the Thursday practice. Will JT tell Ricky the truth or keep lying?
3. At the end of the scene, have JT tell how he feels about the conversation.

> A **scene** is one part or section of a play, taking place in one location at one time.

Dialogue

- Your characters should sound like real people.
- The language characters use should reflect their age and the situation.
- Characters don't have to speak in complete sentences, but all sentences should still make sense to your reader.
- Read your dialogue aloud when you finish writing to check how it sounds.

D

LANGUAGE CONVENTIONS *Common Errors: Sentence Fragments*

- A **sentence fragment** is a group of words that looks like a sentence but does not express a complete thought.
  EXAMPLE: <u>A rail slide</u>. This sentence is incomplete because it is just a phrase. There is no one completing an action.

- A sentence fragment can be corrected by adding the missing information to it.
  EXAMPLE: <u>I know how to do</u> a rail slide.

- Writers often use sentence fragments in **dialogue**. In **formal** writing, however, sentence fragments should not be used.

1. <u>Underline</u> **one** sentence fragment in "Skate Secrets." In the margin, rewrite the sentence fragment as a complete sentence.
2. <u>Underline</u> the sentence fragments below. In your notebook, rewrite the sentences correctly.

   a. Jumped high into the air on his board.

   b. Reached the top and flipped off the board.

   c. I love watching skateboarding. My definition of exciting.

   d. It was the first time I had been to a skateboarding meet. Awesome riding.

   e. JT learns all the hardest skateboarding moves. In fact, the best skateboarder ever.

3. In your notebook, describe how you decided whether a sentence was complete or not.

Before Reading

Think about your favourite subject in school. What is it about that subject that makes you like it the best? Think about the subject that you like the least. What is it about that subject that makes you like it the least?

Everyone learns in different ways. How do you think you learn best? Take this quiz to find out.

What's Your Learning Style?

QUIZ from *Psychology for Kids* by Jonni Kincher

To learn, you depend on your senses to bring information to your brain. Most people tend to use one of their senses more than the others. Some people learn best by listening. They are called **auditory learners**. Other people learn best by reading or seeing pictures. They are **visual learners**. Still others learn best by touching and doing things. They are called **kinesthetic learners**.

Scientists and <u>psychologists</u> don't know why people use one sense more than the others. Maybe the sense they use the most just works better for them. Knowing your learning style may help you to learn. It may also explain why some things just don't make sense to you.

Complete this quiz. For each question, circle the first answer that comes to your mind. Don't spend too much time thinking about any question.

> **VOCABULARY**
>
> **psychologists:** people trained in the study of the mind and the ways of thought. Psychology tries to explain why people act, think, and feel as they do.

> **GOALS AT A GLANCE**
>
> explaining information • making connections

1. In which way would you rather learn how a computer works?
   a. by watching a movie about it
   b. by listening to someone explain it
   c. by taking the computer apart and trying to figure it out for yourself

2. Which would you prefer to read for fun?
   a. a travel book with a lot of pictures in it
   b. a mystery book with a lot of conversation in it
   c. a book where you answer questions and do puzzles

3. When you aren't sure how to spell a word, which of these are you most likely to do?
   a. write it out to see if it looks right
   b. sound it out
   c. write it out to sense if it feels right

4. If you were at a party, what would you be most likely to remember the next day?
   a. the faces of the people there, but not the names
   b. the names but not the faces
   c. the things you did and said while you were there

5. How would you rather study for a test?
   a. read notes, read headings in a book, or look at diagrams and illustrations
   b. have someone ask you questions or repeat facts silently to yourself
   c. write things out on index cards and make models or diagrams

6. When you see the word **dog**, what do you do first?
   a. think of a picture of a particular dog
   b. say the word **dog** to yourself silently
   c. sense the feeling of being with a dog (petting it or running with it)

7. What do you find most distracting when you are trying to concentrate?
   a. visual distractions
   b. noises
   c. other sensations like hunger, tight shoes, or worry

8. How do you prefer to solve a problem?
   a. make a list, organize the steps, and check them off as they are done
   b. make a few phone calls and talk to friends or experts
   c. make a model of the problem or walk through all the steps in your mind

9. Which are you most likely to do while standing in a long line at the movies?
   a. look at the posters advertising other movies
   b. talk to the person next to you
   c. tap your foot or move around in some other way

10. You have just entered a science museum. What will you do first?
   a. look around and find a map showing the locations of the various exhibits
   b. talk to a museum guide and ask about exhibits
   c. go into the first exhibit that looks interesting and read directions later

11. When you are angry, which are you most likely to do?
   a. scowl
   b. shout or "blow up"
   c. stomp off and slam doors

12. When you are happy, what are you most likely to do?
   a. grin
   b. shout with joy
   c. jump for joy

13. Which would you rather go to?
   a. an art class
   b. a music class
   c. an exercise class

14. Which of these do you do when you listen to music?
   a. daydream (see images that go with the music)
   b. hum along
   c. move with the music, clap, or tap your foot

15. How would you rather tell a story?
   a. write it out
   b. tell it out loud
   c. act it out

16. Which restaurant would you rather **not** go to?
   a. one with the lights too bright
   b. one with the music too loud
   c. one with uncomfortable chairs

WHAT'S YOUR STYLE?

Add up your a's, b's, and c's:

a's _____ b's _____ c's _____

- If you scored mostly a's, you may be a **visual learner** (that is, have a visual learning style). You learn by reading and seeing.
- If you scored mostly b's, you may be an **auditory learner** (that is, have an auditory learning style). You learn by hearing and listening.
- If you had mostly c's, you may be a **kinesthetic learner** (that is, have a kinesthetic learning style). You learn by touching and doing.
- If your score was about the same for two or more letters, you depend on more than one learning style.

It's common to use different learning styles for different tasks. For instance, you might repeat your German lessons out loud to prepare for a test, but study your textbook to prepare for your math quiz. And you might repeat some experiments you did in class to prepare for your chemistry test.

In these cases, you're using an auditory learning style to learn a language. You're using a visual learning style to learn math. You're using a kinesthetic learning style to learn chemistry. Each one helps you learn what you need to know.

AFTER THE QUIZ

- The next time you study for a quiz or test, put into practise what you learned in this quiz. If your learning style is auditory, read out loud the information you need to know. If it's kinesthetic, make a model or do something practical that will help you learn the information. If it's visual, read a text and study illustrations.
- If you have to do a project in school, design one that fits your learning style.

Type of Learner	This Type Learns Best By
Visual Learner	• reading • seeing (pictures, photos, maps, charts) • watching (videos, other people) • drawing • making diagrams
Auditory Learner	• listening (to experts, radio, tapes, self) • talking with others • reading out loud
Kinesthetic Learner	• touching • doing things • making things • moving

If you liked this quiz, look for the book *Psychology for Kids: 40 Fun Tests that Help You Learn About Yourself* by Jonni Kincher.

UNDERSTANDING THE SELECTION *Explaining Information*

1. Return to the questions you answered in "Before Reading" on page 57. Now that you've read this selection, can you explain why one subject is your favourite and the other is your least favourite?

   _____

   _____

2. What other questions do you have about learning styles?

   _____

   _____

3. Would you like to read other selections like this one? Why or why not?

   _____

   _____

B ## CRITICAL THINKING *Making Connections*

1. Complete the following Problem/Solution chart by suggesting **three** different ways riding a bike can be taught. You need to use each of the three different learning styles.

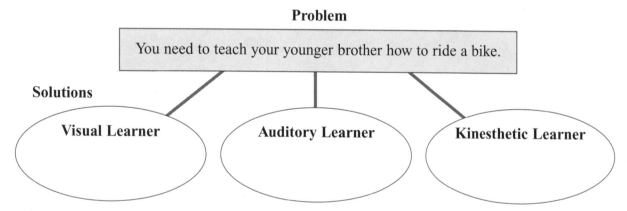

Problem

You need to teach your younger brother how to ride a bike.

Solutions

Visual Learner   Auditory Learner   Kinesthetic Learner

2. Complete the chart below by providing **one** example of when you have used a particular learning style in the past, and **one** example of when you might use it in the future.

Learning Style	Past	Future
Visual Learning Style		
Auditory Learning Style		
Kinesthetic Learning Style		

C RESEARCHING *Identifying Resources*

1. Think about your strongest learning style. For that learning style, what type of resources should you use when you have a research project to complete at school?
2. Fill in the chart for your strongest learning style, choosing suggestions from the box below. What are the best resources for you to use? Can some resources fit more than one learning style? Explain your answer.
3. With a small group, discuss this chart. What other resources would you add to the list?

Learning Style	Good Resources for That Style
Visual Learning Style	
Auditory Learning Style	
Kinesthetic Learning Style	

maps	experts	charts/diagrams	encyclopedias	movies/videos
models	dictionaries	newspapers	Internet sites	other students
talking books	magazines	dioramas	tools	slides/photos
experiments	posters	teachers/librarians	collages	samples

EXTENDING: Make a plan for your next project, based on your learning style.

D LANGUAGE CONVENTIONS *Pronouns*

- A **pronoun** is a word used in place of a noun (for information on nouns see page 5).
  EXAMPLES: you, they, me, I, he, it, who, this

Complete these sentences by choosing the right pronoun.

1. Chris and Joe have forgotten that _____ need their books for the test. (they, he, it)

2. _____ left my sweater in the car. (I, He, She)

3. Do _____ remember where to go? (you, she, it)

4. When does _____ plan to hand in her project? (he, she, I)

5. Will _____ need our calculators? (I, they, we)

Before Reading

Have you ever played the game "Broken Telephone"? That's a game where one person whispers a sentence to a second person. The second person whispers the sentence to a third person and so on. What do you think happens to that original sentence?

Think about what happens when you tell a friend a secret or something personal, and they tell another friend.

How do you feel about gossip?

MESSAGE MIX-UPS

A STORY THROUGH VOICE MESSAGES by Diane Robitaille

Hi! You've reached Wayne. I can't take your call right now. Please leave a message, and I'll get back to you later. BEEEP.

Hi Wayne, it's Mike. Can you believe it? My parents are sending me to stay with my aunt in Québec while they go to Italy this summer! At least she works for Cirque du Soleil. That's pretty cool. Well, I have to go pack.

Hello, you've reached Tom, Mary, and Steve. We can't come to the phone right now. Please leave a message at the beep. BEEEP.

Hey Steve, it's Wayne. Have you heard? Mike's parents are sending him to Italy to join a circus. How lucky can you get? I don't know what he'll be doing, training lions maybe. Ha!

GOALS AT A GLANCE

sequencing • performing the selection

Hello, you have reached Kelly, Wanda, and Greg. We're not able to take your call right now. Please leave a message at the tone. BEEEP.

Hi Wanda, this is Steve. Have you heard? Mike is going to be a lion tamer in a circus in Italy. I always thought he would be better at getting shot from a cannon!

Hi, you've reached Lara. I can't come to the phone right now. Please leave a message at the beep. BEEEP.

Hi Lara. It's Wanda. You'll never believe this: Mike got a job in Rome! He's getting shot from a cannon over the heads of lions. He's going to be there for months. I thought he was supposed to be teaching you to scuba dive this summer?

Hello, you have reached Mike. I can't take your call right now. Please leave a message. BEEEP.

Hey Mike! It's Lara. What's going on? Is it true you've got a job in Rome this summer taking care of lions at the zoo? You promised to teach me to scuba dive. We're supposed to go explore that wreck near my cottage.

Beep. Hi, you've reached Lara. I can't come to the phone right now. Please leave a message at the beep. BEEEP.

Hi Lara, it's Mike. What? Who told you that? I don't have a job in Rome this summer. My parents are sending me to Québec to stay with my aunt, but I've got them to agree to let me stay with your family for two weeks. Get back to me and let me know who's spreading these crazy rumours!

1. Put the following statements in the correct order by numbering them 1 to 6.

_____ Wayne leaves a message for Steve, telling him that Mike is joining a circus in Italy.

_____ Mike leaves a message for Lara, explaining what he's really doing.

_____ Wanda leaves a message for Lara, telling her Mike will be working in a circus in Rome.

_____ Lara leaves a message for Mike, asking why he'll be taking care of lions in a zoo in Rome.

_____ Mike leaves a message for Wayne, saying he'll be spending the summer with his aunt in Québec while his parents are in Italy.

_____ Steve leaves a message for Wanda, telling her Mike is going to be a lion tamer in Italy.

2. Check your answers by skimming the selection.

EXTENDING: Each time someone left a message, the person listening to it got confused. Turn back to pages 63 and 64. For each message (except the last one), underline the words that you think caused the confusion.

B CRITICAL THINKING *Elaborating on the Events*

Work with a partner to take turns role-playing one of the characters leaving a message.

1. Reread a message, and then role-play the person leaving that message. **Elaborate** on the message. For example, pretend you are Mike and you're leaving a message for Wayne. Tell Wayne all about your parents' trip and your aunt in Québec.
2. In role as the person **returning** the phone call, your partner now asks you questions about your message. Answer those questions in role.

Reflecting

3. **a.** Does elaborating the messages increase your understanding of the story? Explain.

_____

_____

b. In your opinion, if each character had left a more detailed message in the first place, would there have been any confusion about what Mike was really doing? Explain.

_____

_____

ORAL COMMUNICATION *Performing a Selection*

Work with four classmates to complete this activity. You need enough actors to take on the roles of Mike, Wayne, Steve, Wanda, and Lara.

1. Discuss the selection. As a group, decide which role each member will act out. Remember that actors need to read not only the message they leave but also their answering machine message.
2. Read over your messages. Think about how you will speak your words (angry, happy, surprised, and so on).
3. Together with your group, practise reading the messages. You want your performance to be smooth.
4. When you are ready, create a tape recording of your reading. You could also give a live presentation to your class.

Performing a Selection

- Speak clearly.
- Use the volume and tone of your voice to indicate how the character is feeling. Practise speaking the lines with different tones or volumes to see what sounds best for each line.
- Think about where you place the emphasis in a word or sentence.
  For example, the impact of the following sentence changes slightly when emphasis is put on the words **my aunt** instead of **in Québec**:

  My parents are sending me to stay with my aunt in Québec.

EXTENDING: With your group, talk about some common rules for leaving voice messages. For example, some people always leave their phone number or give the date and time they are calling.

 D

WRITING *A Story Through Messages*

Use "Message Mix-Ups" as a model to write a story. Follow these steps.

1. Think of a situation that can be the basis for the story. You need a reason for the first phone call. For example, maybe the main character is moving away or has just been given a puppy.
2. Think about the other characters. Are they family, friends, or strangers?
3. Think about how each character is feeling. Use words and punctuation that show those feelings.
4. Write at least **four** messages.

EXTENDING: Give a live performance of your story for your class or create a tape recording to share with classmates.

Instead of the above activity, you could write a **sequel** to "Message Mix-Ups," a series of messages continuing the story.

During Reading
"Yesterday"

Personal Connections

When you make **personal connections** to a text you tell your thoughts and feelings about a poem or story.
- Make connections between the writing and your own life.
- Write what you think about the writer's ideas.
- Explain why you think as you do about the selection.
- Use examples from the selection to support your ideas.

Step 1. Read the poem once and then make notes in the margins around the poem.

    a. Write down any thoughts about the poem that come into your mind.

    b. Comment on how the poem is written. For example, note the use of repetition, things the poet describes, how the poem appeals to your sense of sight, hearing, or taste.

    c. Label your favourite parts of the poem.

    d. Write down any questions you have about the poem.

Step 2. Use the notes you made to write a one-paragraph personal response to the poem.

_____

_____

_____

_____

_____

_____

_____

_____

_____

Further Reading

If you like this poem, you can read other poems by Canadian author Jean Little in her book *Hey World, Here I Am!*

    Jean has written many books for children and young adults. She is almost blind and has a talking computer to help her write.

Yesterday

POEM from *Hey World, Here I Am!* by Jean Little

Yesterday I knew all the answers
Or I knew my parents did.

Yesterday I had my Best Friend
And my Second Best Friend
And I knew whose Best Friend I was
And who disliked me.

Yesterday I hated asparagus and coconut and parsnips
And mustard and pickles and olives
And anything I'd never tasted.

Yesterday I knew what was Right and what was Wrong
And I never had any trouble deciding which was which.
It always seemed so obvious.

But today…everything's changing.
I suddenly have a million unanswered questions.
Everybody I meet might become a friend.
I tried eating snails with garlic sauce—and I liked them!
And I know the delicate shadings that lie between
Good and evil—and I face their dilemma.
Life is harder now…and yet, easier…
And more and more exciting!

VOCABULARY

dilemma: a serious problem

GOALS AT A GLANCE

making comparisons • thinking about poetry

UNDERSTANDING THE SELECTION *Making Comparisons*

1. The poem compares "yesterday" and "today." Circle the words **yesterday** and **today** everywhere they appear in the poem. Draw a line to separate the two parts of the poem.

2. Read each statement below. Label it **yesterday** or **today** based on when the speaker feels that way.

   a. The speaker feels life is harder. _____

   b. The speaker feels everyone might become a friend. _____

   c. The speaker has all the answers. _____

   d. The speaker has a million questions. _____

   e. The speaker knows there is a grey area between good and evil. _____

   f. The speaker knows right and wrong. _____

   g. The speaker has a best friend. _____

B CRITICAL THINKING *Thinking About Poetry*

1. Who is the **speaker** of the poem? The speaker of the poem is probably about _____ years

   old. The clues in the poem about the speaker's age are _____

   _____ .

2. Who is the **audience** the speaker is talking to? (Hint: The audience can be the speaker

   himself or herself or another person.) I think the audience of the poem is _____

   because _____

   _____ .

3. What is the poem **about**? The speaker is describing the differences between _____

   and _____ .

4. a. What **feelings** does the poem express? The speaker is feeling _____

   _____ .

   b. Circle some of the words in the poem that show these feelings.

5. What **ideas** about life or people's behaviour is the poet exploring? The poet is exploring

   _____ .

C   WRITING *Poetry*

1. Use "Yesterday" as a model. Think about what you learned about poetry in activity B on page 69.

2. Describe what you were like "yesterday" and what you are like "today." Create a chart like this one to help you organize your ideas. List at least **five** items for each column.

Yesterday	Today

3. Choose strong words to describe yourself. Think about what you learned about yourself as you completed this unit.

4. Exchange poems with a partner. Read and discuss your descriptions.

D   LANGUAGE CONVENTIONS *Possessive Pronouns*

> • **Possessive pronouns** show ownership of something: mine, yours, his, hers, its, ours, theirs.
>   EXAMPLES: The house was <u>theirs</u>. (**theirs** = belonged to **them**)

1. Complete these sentences with the correct possessive pronoun from the list above.

   a. She has a scarf just like _____ .

   b. These gloves are not my gloves. Philippe, are they _____ ?

   c. We've taken our vitamins. Has Melanie taken _____ ?

> • Some possessive pronouns act as adjectives: my, your, his, her, its, our, their
>   EXAMPLE: I went to <u>their</u> house. (**Their** modifies the noun **house**)

2. Circle the correct possessive pronoun in each sentence.

   a. Yesterday I saw **my/mine** best friend.

   b. My father serves **ours/our** favourite dessert every Friday.

   c. Claire had **her/hers** bike stolen last week.

> • Never use an apostrophe (') with a possessive pronoun.
>   EXAMPLES: The dog buried <u>its</u> bone in the yard. Is this book <u>yours</u>?

UNIT 3 WRAP-UP

SELF-ASSESSMENT *Writing Activities*

1. Choose **one** writing activity listed below. In your notebook, explain what you have learned about completing that activity.

   - ❏ writing dialogue
   - ❏ correcting sentence fragments
   - ❏ writing a story through messages
   - ❏ writing a personal response
   - ❏ writing a poem

2. Think about all the writing activities you completed in this unit. Which activity do you think you completed most successfully? Why? What do you think helped you succeed (preparation, organization, creative thinking, or something else)?

   _____

   _____

   _____

PROJECT IDEA *Script*

Work with a small group to create a short script about <u>identity</u>.

Step 1. As a group, discuss the selections you read in the *Identity* unit. What different topics did each selection cover? What other identity topics interest you and your group? Record your ideas.

Step 2. Choose **one** identity topic as the focus for your script. Brainstorm thoughts and feelings about this topic. Think about how you can explore these ideas in your script.

Step 3. Use the outline at right to help you plan your script. Use "Skate Secrets" (page 53) as a model.

Step 4. Together, write your script. As you work, read the dialogue out loud to make sure it sounds realistic. Review the writing strategies on page 56.

Step 5. Practise performing your script. Use the performing strategies on page 66. When you are happy with your performance, present your script to the class.

> **OUTLINE**
>
> **Characters** (who)
> -
> -
> -
>
> **Setting** (where and when)
> -
>
> **Conflict** (what's the problem)
> -
>
> **Plot** (what happens)
> -
> -
>
> **Ending** (how is the problem solved?)
> -

What should you do when you are asked to make personal connections to a selection? Begin by reading it carefully. Write your comments about the selection either in the margin or on another piece of paper. (Remember, everyone's personal connections with a poem will be different, because they're personal!)

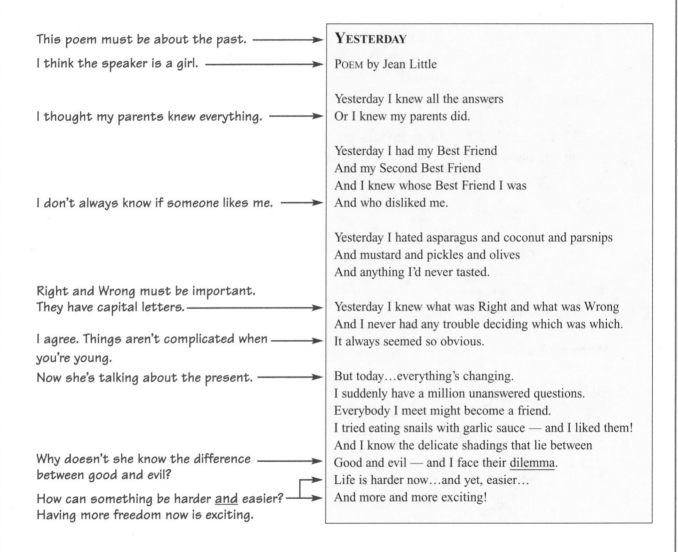

This poem must be about the past. ⟶

I think the speaker is a girl. ⟶

I thought my parents knew everything. ⟶

I don't always know if someone likes me. ⟶

Right and Wrong must be important. They have capital letters. ⟶

I agree. Things aren't complicated when you're young. ⟶

Now she's talking about the present. ⟶

Why doesn't she know the difference between good and evil? ⟶

How can something be harder and easier? Having more freedom now is exciting. ⟶

YESTERDAY

POEM by Jean Little

Yesterday I knew all the answers
Or I knew my parents did.

Yesterday I had my Best Friend
And my Second Best Friend
And I knew whose Best Friend I was
And who disliked me.

Yesterday I hated asparagus and coconut and parsnips
And mustard and pickles and olives
And anything I'd never tasted.

Yesterday I knew what was Right and what was Wrong
And I never had any trouble deciding which was which.
It always seemed so obvious.

But today…everything's changing.
I suddenly have a million unanswered questions.
Everybody I meet might become a friend.
I tried eating snails with garlic sauce — and I liked them!
And I know the delicate shadings that lie between
Good and evil — and I face their dilemma.
Life is harder now…and yet, easier…
And more and more exciting!

After you have written your comments, organize your ideas into a paragraph.

In "Yesterday," I think the speaker is contrasting what she was like "yesterday" with what she is like "today." I think the most important point is that "yesterday" she found it easy to know Right from Wrong. Now she's a teenager, and everything has changed. She's even confused about good and evil. I think Jean Little really understands how life gets complicated when you become a teenager.

Before Reading
"E-Communications Timeline"

The next selection provides a timeline for some major developments in **electronic communications technology** (technology that deals with inventions like the telephone, computer, or radio).

Look at the electronic inventions listed in the box. Can you guess which one was invented first? Which one was invented last? Place the inventions on the flowchart in the order in which you think they were invented.

personal computer	radio	e-mail	telephone
World Wide Web	TV	computer	satellites

1.

↓

2.

↓

3.

↓

4.

↓

5.

↓

6.

↓

7.

↓

8.

As you read the selection, check the flowchart.
Make corrections, if necessary.

During Reading

This selection uses some technical **jargon**.
As you read, <u>underline</u> the jargon in the selection.

> **Jargon** is the language of a particular group or profession. For example, **medical jargon** refers to terms commonly used by doctors or nurses, terms such as **abrasion** rather than **scrape**, or **contusion** rather than **bruise**. Jargon is sometimes so complicated that it makes communication unclear.

E-Communications Timeline

TIMELINE by David Jefferis

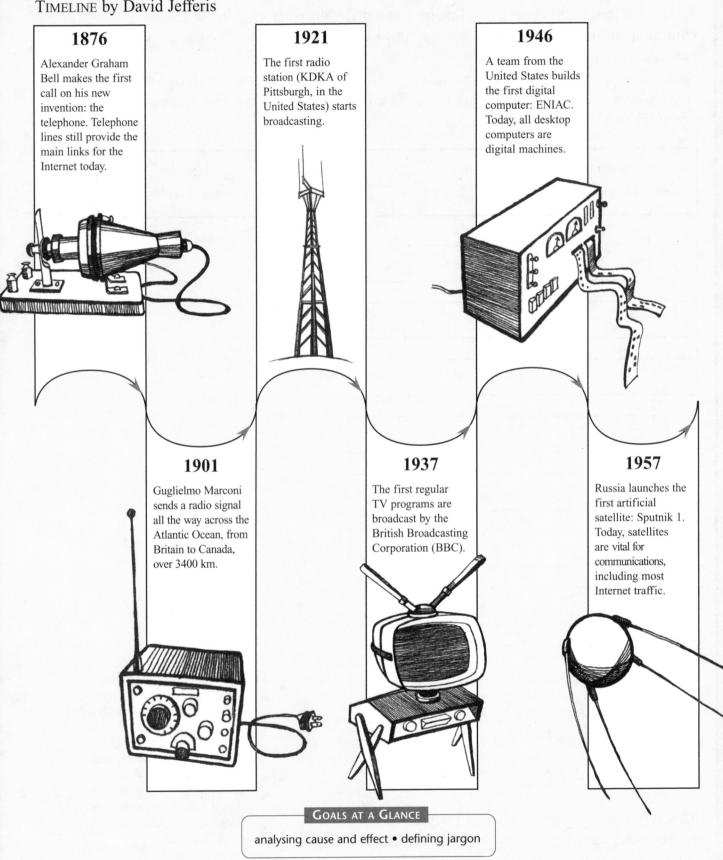

1876

Alexander Graham Bell makes the first call on his new invention: the telephone. Telephone lines still provide the main links for the Internet today.

1921

The first radio station (KDKA of Pittsburgh, in the United States) starts broadcasting.

1946

A team from the United States builds the first digital computer: ENIAC. Today, all desktop computers are digital machines.

1901

Guglielmo Marconi sends a radio signal all the way across the Atlantic Ocean, from Britain to Canada, over 3400 km.

1937

The first regular TV programs are broadcast by the British Broadcasting Corporation (BBC).

1957

Russia launches the first artificial satellite: Sputnik 1. Today, satellites are vital for communications, including most Internet traffic.

GOALS AT A GLANCE

analysing cause and effect • defining jargon

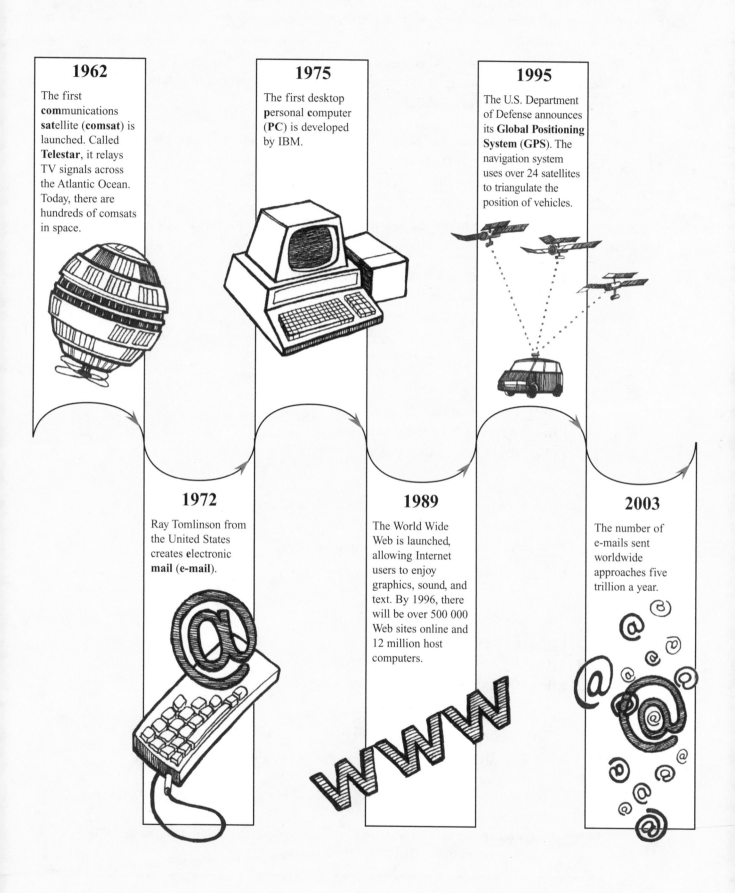

1962

The first **com**munications **sat**ellite (**comsat**) is launched. Called **Telestar**, it relays TV signals across the Atlantic Ocean. Today, there are hundreds of comsats in space.

1975

The first desktop **p**ersonal **c**omputer (**PC**) is developed by IBM.

1995

The U.S. Department of Defense announces its **Global Positioning System** (**GPS**). The navigation system uses over 24 satellites to triangulate the position of vehicles.

1972

Ray Tomlinson from the United States creates **e**lectronic **mail** (**e-mail**).

1989

The World Wide Web is launched, allowing Internet users to enjoy graphics, sound, and text. By 1996, there will be over 500 000 Web sites online and 12 million host computers.

2003

The number of e-mails sent worldwide approaches five trillion a year.

- When one event happens, it sometimes causes another event to happen. This is called **cause and effect**. For example, when rain falls for a long time, puddles form.

    Cause Rain → Effect Puddles

- A cause can have more than one effect. For example, rain can also cause plants to grow.

    Cause Rain → Effect Puddles
              → Effect Plants grow

Read each cause statement below. Check off each effect that you think follows that statement.

Cause In 1876, Alexander Graham Bell invents the telephone.
- ❏ Effect People no longer visit one another.
- ❏ Effect People keep in touch with relatives far away.
- ❏ Effect Phoning to have a pizza delivered eventually becomes possible.

Cause In 1921, the first radio station starts broadcasting.
- ❏ Effect People buy radios.
- ❏ Effect Writers start writing radio plays.
- ❏ Effect People read more books.

Cause In 1957, Russia launches the first artificial satellite.
- ❏ Effect Many parents name their child "Sputnik."
- ❏ Effect Satellites are used for communications.
- ❏ Effect More satellites are launched.

Cause In 1989, the World Wide Web is launched.
- ❏ Effect Computer sales go down.
- ❏ Effect More Web sites are developed.
- ❏ Effect Companies start selling items on the Internet.

Critical Thinking Strategies

Analysing Cause and Effect

- To analyse cause-and-effect relationships, first identify the cause (for example, rain).
- Then identify the effect or effects caused by that initial event (for example, puddles, plants grow).
- You can use arrows to represent cause-and-effect relationships, as in the cause-and-effect chart above.

B VOCABULARY *Defining Jargon*

1. Reread the definition of **jargon** on page 73.
2. Compare the jargon you underlined in "E-communications Timeline" with the jargon underlined by a classmate. Discuss the meaning of those words.
3. For **two** of the terms you underlined, write a definition below.

    a. _____

    b. _____

EXTENDING: As you read the next selection, "Teens Log on to Stay Connected," circle all the jargon. Discuss how much of the jargon (such as **surf**, **net**, **cyberspace**) in the selection is now part of the everyday speech of many people.

C MEDIA *Investigating E-Communications*

1. Use the library to locate more information on e-communications technology.
2. Write **three** new entries to add to the selection. Add your entries where they belong on the timeline.

Date: _____ Event: _____

_____

Date: _____ Event: _____

_____

Date: _____ Event: _____

_____

TIPS

Library Research

- Use the library computer catalogue to locate books on your research topic.
- Focus your search by using keywords from your topic, for example: **computers**, **communications**, or **TV**.
- A list of books will come up on the screen. Find the books on the library shelves by using the call numbers of the books.
- You may find other useful books on your topic in the same area on the shelf.

- A **verb** is a word that expresses an action or a state of being.

  EXAMPLES: make, open, provide, send, start, think, be, build, launch, relay, develop, enjoy, seem, find

---

1. Underline the verbs in the sentences below.

   a. In the year 1975, IBM developed the first personal computer.

   b. Today, desktop computers are digital machines.

   c. By 1996, there were over 500 000 Web sites online.

   d. BBC broadcast the first regular TV shows in 1937.

   e. Kent has his own e-mail address.

- **Vivid verbs** are strong, descriptive verbs. They give the reader a better understanding of what is happening. Using vivid verbs in your writing can increase its power.

  EXAMPLES: My brother <u>shouted</u> at the charging dog.

  My brother <u>bellowed</u> at the charging dog.

---

2. To complete each sentence, choose the **most** vivid verb in brackets. Think about how the meaning of the sentence changes as you use different words.

   a. Cassie _____ home. (ran, jogged, dashed, bolted)

   b. Mike _____ his new kitten. (likes, loves, adores)

   c. Rajiv _____ his parents for a computer. (begged, asked)

   d. The car _____ into flames. (burst, erupted, exploded)

   e. Erin _____ for her stolen bike. (hunted, looked, searched)

3. With a classmate, compare and discuss your answers in question 2. Your opinion about the most vivid verb may not be the same as your partner's opinion.

EXTENDING: Write a paragraph about one e-communications invention and its effect on your life. Read over your paragraph and replace at least **five** verbs with more vivid ones.

Before Reading
"Teens Log On to Stay Connected"

Read the following statements about how young people use the Internet. Decide whether each one is **true** or **false**. In the space provided, explain why you think so.

1. Most young people spend about 20 hours a week on the Internet. _____

    _____

2. Boys and girls spend their time on the Internet very differently. _____

    _____

3. Boys and girls spend the same amount of time on the Internet. _____

    _____

4. When they're on the Internet, young people spend all of their time playing games. _____

    _____

5. If you have made friends with other teens on the Internet, it is **not** a good idea to give them

    your phone number. _____

    _____

During Reading

The selection provides statistics comparing the Internet behaviour of teens in the years 2000 and 2001. As you read, fill out the chart below.

Internet Behaviour of Teens	In 2000	In 2001
Percentage with computers who surf the Internet at home		
Percentage with Internet access		
Percentage with own e-mail address		
Hours spent on the Internet each week		

Teens LOG ON to Stay Connected

PRESS RELEASE from Corus Entertainment
Toronto, Wednesday, December 5, 2001

Every year YTV completes a survey to find out how young people use the Internet and other media. This year YTV reports that 72% of Canada's teens with computers are surfing the Internet from the comfort of their home. That's a significant increase from 62% in the year 2000.

This annual national survey tracks the lifestyles, attitudes, and behaviour of young people. It reports that 84% of teens have access to the Internet, whether at home, school, or library. That's up from 75% last year. Using the Internet to communicate has become an important pastime. Over half of teens (51%) who surf the Internet have their own personal e-mail address, a big increase from 35% the year before.

Teens are also spending more time online, an average of 4.9 hours per week compared to 3.8 hours in 2000. And for the first time, this year, girls are spending more time (5 hours per week) on the Internet than boys (4.8 hours).

Julie Look, the Director of Research of Corus Entertainment, says, "Whether they are exploring Web sites, playing games, chatting with friends, or doing research on school projects, the Internet is an essential tool for teens."

How are teens spending their time online? Using the Internet to learn and gather information tops the list of teens' online activities. In order of priority, teens spend most of their time in cyberspace looking for information and checking out Web sites, followed by researching school projects, playing online games, sending e-mails, and using ICQ for instant messaging.

GOALS AT A GLANCE

summarizing • creating a poster

Aside from researching, girls and boys spend their time online differently. Boys like to spend their time playing online games, followed by sending e-mails, downloading music, and chatting in chat rooms. Girls consider communication their top priority with sending e-mails at the top of their list, followed by playing online games and chatting in chat rooms.

Most parents are concerned about how their children use the Internet, with 31% very concerned. Although most parents say they sometimes surf the Net with their teens, a third of parents have installed a device to make sure that their kids only have access to information that is appropriate.

WEB SAFETY

Tips from the Royal Canadian Mounted Police Web Site

1. Be aware that people may not be who they say they are on the Internet. An adult could pretend to be a kid your age just to get to know you. Sometimes they can do this over a long period of time to develop your trust.

2. Do not give out or send personal information such as your address, your phone number, where you go to school, or photos to someone that you only know through the Internet unless you have your parents' or guardian's permission. Do not give out any information that you shouldn't give to a stranger in a park, on the telephone, or anywhere else.

3. Do not agree to meet people that you have met through the Internet until you check with your parents or guardian, and be sure that your parents or guardian attend the first couple of meetings with you. The first meeting should always be in a public place.

4. Do not respond to any messages that ask for personal information, messages that are mean, or messages that make you feel uncomfortable. You do not have to continue. Sign off and surf off to somewhere else.

5. Talk to your parents or guardian about setting up some rules to ensure that your use of the Internet will be rewarding, fun, and safe. Get your parents involved and show them how much fun the Internet can be.

A UNDERSTANDING THE SELECTION *Locating Information*

1. Listed in the first column of this chart are the five statements you responded to before reading the selection. Read these statements again.
2. Now that you have read the selection, answer these questions using your knowledge of the selection. Record **true** or **false** in the second column.
3. In the third column, record evidence from "Teens Log on to Stay Connected" to support your answer.

Statement from page 79	True or False?	Evidence from Selection
Most young people spend about 20 hours a week on the Internet.		
Boys and girls spend their time on the Internet very differently.		
Boys and girls spend the same amount of time on the Internet.		
When they're on the Internet, young people spend all of their time playing games.		
If you have made friends with other teens on the Internet, it is **not** a good idea to give them your phone number.		

B CRITICAL THINKING *Summarizing*

1. Check off the **three** sentences below that you think best **summarize** "Teens Log On to Stay Connected."

   > To **summarize** is to make a brief statement giving the main points of a text.

   ❏ Boys and girls both enjoy chat rooms.
   ❏ Boys and girls spend the same amount of time on the Internet.
   ❏ In the year 2000, 35% of teens had an e-mail address.
   ❏ Canada's teens are spending more time online.
   ❏ Julie Look works for Corus Entertainment.
   ❏ Most teens have high-speed Internet service.
   ❏ Teens spend most of their time online looking for information.

2. Write a one-sentence summary for each tip in "Web Safety." You can write each of your summary sentences on page 81 beside the tip.

1. Do you find this comic strip funny? Why or why not? _____

_____

2. Read the following statement:

   The comic strip explores the conflict between generations, between a father's knowledge and a child's understanding of that knowledge.

   Do you agree with this statement? Why or why not? _____

   _____

   _____

3. What else could the father say or do to help the son understand the purpose of a letter

   opener? _____

   _____

4. How has technology changed the way we communicate? Suggest **one** way. _____

   _____

5. What is **one** advantage of new technologies? _____

   _____

6. What is **one** disadvantage of new technologies? _____

   _____

EXTENDING: Use your ideas from question 3 or 4 to develop another comic strip for these characters.

VISUAL COMMUNICATION *Creating a Poster*

Follow these steps to create a poster about Web safety for kids aged six to ten. The purpose of your poster is to inform.

1. Rewrite your summary sentences from activity B2 for a younger audience. Use these on your poster.
2. Choose colours and visuals that will appeal to your intended audience.
3. After you have finished your poster, test it on several kids aged six to ten. Ask questions to help you find out whether they "get the message."

4. Share your poster and your feedback with a group of classmates. Discuss your results.

E LANGUAGE CONVENTIONS *Present Tense*

- The **tense** of a verb tells the **time** (present, past, or future) of the action, feeling, or state of being. The **present tense** tells what is happening now or tells about an ongoing action.
  EXAMPLES: Jared <u>knows</u> the answer to this question. (happening now)
  Michaela always <u>guesses</u> the answer. (ongoing action)

- When you are reading a selection, pay attention to the verb tense that the author is using. Think about what the verb tense tells you about the action or selection.

1. <u>Underline</u> the verb in the present tense in each sentence below.

   a. Jackie reads all about the new computer game.

   b. Ray launches his new Web site.

   c. I love science class most of all.

   d. You need a new computer.

   e. They know the password for my computer.

- The present tense is often used in timelines, captions, or reports.
  EXAMPLES: The first radio station <u>starts</u> broadcasting.
  The survey <u>reports</u> that 84% of teens have Internet access.

2. Write **two** sentences describing how you use the Internet. Use the present tense.

_____

_____

_____

Before Reading

What is your favourite TV show? _____

What do you like about it? _____

_____

If you could change one thing about the show, what would you change? Explain why.

_____

_____

Behind the Scenes with a TV Tester

INTERVIEW from *The TV Book* by Shelagh Wallace

What's it like to be involved in the testing of TV shows? Just ask Goody Gerner. Goody is the president and owner of Generations Research Incorporated, a company that uses kids to test products, advertising ideas, and TV shows. Goody and her company have played an important role in helping make some good TV shows even better.

In the following interview she answers some common questions about her job and her company.

Interviewer: When you're testing a kids' TV show, what does the <u>network</u> expect you to do?

Goody: It really depends on what stage the network is at with the show. Sometimes the show is at the <u>idea stage</u>, before they've even shot anything, and we find out what kids think about the idea. Sometimes we play tapes of the actors auditioning for the show to see who kids like the best.

GOALS AT A GLANCE

using a flowchart • drawing conclusions

Interviewer: What do you actually do when you're testing a TV show with kids?

Goody: We'll usually test with about five or six kids at a time. The kids come to a central location, usually a place that has a room with a one-way mirror. The kids inside the room can't see out through the mirror. The people from the network sit outside the room and look through the mirror to see how the kids are reacting to the TV show. I usually leave the room and watch the kids through the mirror too. If I'm in the room, the kids are on their best behaviour and watch the TV show. But if I leave the room, they sometimes lose attention, make comments, and talk to each other. It's important we find out their real response to the show.

Interviewer: Do the kids know there are people on the other side of the mirror watching them?

Goody: Yes, you have to tell them. But they forget, almost immediately. Adults forget too. Everybody forgets about the mirror!

Interviewer: What kinds of questions do you ask?

Goody: It depends what we're testing. No matter what I'm testing, I always ask them: What did you like? What didn't you like? What was funny, dumb, cute, boring, exciting? Who is the show most appropriate for: boys or girls? Kids older than you or younger than you? Would you want to watch the show again?

Interviewer: Do the networks look for specific answers to specific questions?

Goody: The networks may have specific things that they're concerned about. For instance, they might want to know how kids feel about the music or the show's set.

Interviewer: What happens after the testing?

Goody: During testing, each group is always taped. Afterward, the network can take the tapes away and study them. I write a report for the network that is my impression of the testing. I back up what I say in the report by including some of the kids' comments from the tapes.

Interviewer: If kids don't like the show, will a network rework it?

Goody: Yes.

Interviewer: How many times can a show go through this process?

Goody: I've tested the same show three or four times. Of the shows I've tested, most end up on TV because we help make them better!

Using a Flowchart

A **flowchart** clearly shows the order of a series of events (the steps in a process, or the sequence of events in a story). A flowchart helps you organize information and makes the information easier to understand.

- Look over all the steps (or events). Think about which one needs to be done first. Put that step in the first box.
- Now, think about what needs to be done next. That step goes in the second box. Repeat this process for each step.
- When you're done, read over the flowchart. Are the steps in a logical order? If the steps don't seem to be in the correct order, rearrange them.

1. What is the correct sequence of events when a TV show is tested? Use the **flowchart** below to organize the following steps in the correct order:

   ✦ The networks study tapes of the kids reacting to the show.
   ✦ The kids go to a central location, a room with a one-way mirror.
   ✦ The network makes the TV show better.
   ✦ The kids answer questions about the show they just saw.
   ✦ The network asks Goody Gerner's company to test a TV show on kids.
   ✦ The kids watch the TV show.

   ↓

   ↓

   ↓

   ↓

   ↓

2. What helped you complete this activity? Write down **one** tip you would give someone else trying to complete this activity. _____

   _____

   _____

1. Choose a popular TV show. Make up **three** questions about it that a researcher like Goody Gerner might ask someone.

The Name of The Show:
Question 1:
Question 2:
Question 3:

2. Use your questions to interview **three** classmates who are familiar with the show.
3. Record their answers.

_____

_____

_____

_____

_____

_____

4. Based on the answers of your classmates, what changes to the show would you recommend? Write down at least **two** suggestions.

_____

_____

_____

Reflecting

5. Should any of your questions be rewritten to make them more effective? If so, how would you change your questions?

_____

_____

TIPS

Forming Questions

- Make sure that your questions are clear and easy to understand.
- Avoid questions that have "yes" or "no" or one word answers.
- Try thinking of some good **why** or **what** questions.
- Make careful notes as you listen to the answers.

- Add an **apostrophe (')** followed by the letter **-s** to show that something belongs to someone. This is known as the **possessive form**.
  EXAMPLES: Goody's company is called Generations Research Incorporated.
  The researcher wrote down the children's answers.

- If a word already ends in the letter **-s**, just add an apostrophe.
  EXAMPLE: Include the kids' comments in your report.

- To check whether you need to use the possessive form, ask yourself whether you mean to say that something belongs to someone.
  CORRECT: The family's TV was broken. (family's TV = the TV belonging to the family)
  CORRECT: Both families went to the movies. (families = more than one family; the word **families** doesn't need an apostrophe because it is a plural, not a possessive.)

- To determine where the apostrophe should go, ask yourself whether one or more people are involved.
  CORRECT: That boy's favourite show was *Star Trek*. (boy's favourite show = the favourite show of one boy)
  CORRECT: Both boys' favourite show was *Star Trek*. (boys' favourite show = the favourite shows of more than one boy)

1. For each sentence, cross out the incorrect word and write the correct possessive form above it. The first one has been done for you.

   Natalie's
   a. ~~Natalies~~ favourite actor was replaced.

   b. Both girls responses were recorded and added up separately.

   c. That networks top show was a courtroom drama.

   d. The boys names on the new show were Taylor and Ashmit.

   e. Last Sunday most peoples radios were tuned to the Super Bowl.

2. In your notebook, write **six** sentences using the following plural words or possessive forms correctly:

   a. kids   **d.** teachers

   b. kid's   **e.** teacher's

   c. kids'   **f.** teachers'

Before Reading

How much TV do you watch each day? How much TV do you think you watch in a week? Do you think your answers are different from the answers of other teens across Canada? Check the following chart to see if you're watching more or less TV than the average person your age.

How Much TV Are Canadians Watching?

CHART from Statistics Canada

AVERAGE HOURS PER WEEK OF TV VIEWING FALL 2001

Province	children 2-11	teens 12-17	adults 18 and over	Total population
	hours per week			
Newfoundland/Labrador	17	16	24	**22**
Prince Edward Island	16	12	21	**20**
Nova Scotia	17	14	26	**24**
New Brunswick	14	14	26	**24**
Québec	15	15	26	**24**
Ontario	14	13	22	**20**
Manitoba	14	13	23	**21**
Saskatchewan	14	13	23	**21**
Alberta	13	13	21	**19**
British Columbia	15	11	23	**21**
Canada	**14**	**13**	**23**	**21**

Source: Statistics Canada
Note: No TV viewing information is available for the Yukon, the Northwest Territories, or Nunavut.

GOALS AT A GLANCE

interpreting charts • conducting a survey

READING *Interpreting Charts*

Charts

- Read the title of the chart and any information around the chart.
- Make sure you understand the type of information the chart is giving you. If you are not sure, ask a classmate or your teacher.
- Read the headings for each column or row.
- Read one row or column at a time.

Study the chart on page 91 and answer the following questions.

1. What information does the chart provide? _____
_____

2. The total population column tells you how many hours of TV is watched by _____
_____.

3. The age group that watches the most TV is _____ .

4. The age group that watches the least TV is _____ .

5. People watch the most TV in these provinces: _____
_____.

6. People watch the least TV in this province: _____ .

7. What strategies did you use to read this chart?
_____
_____
_____

B CRITICAL THINKING *Drawing Conclusions*

1. Answer each of the following questions in your notebook:
   - Why do you think people in some provinces watch less TV than in other provinces? Suggest **one** reason.
   - Why do you think people of a particular age watch more TV than others? Suggest **one** reason.
   - What time of year do you think people watch the most TV? Why?
   - Do you think girls watch more or less TV than boys? Explain your answer.
   - Do you think adults over 60 watch more or less TV than younger adults? Explain.
2. Discuss these questions and your answers in a small group. Do you agree or disagree with the ideas of your classmates? Did your classmates say anything that changed your mind? Explain.

C ORAL COMMUNICATION *Conducting a Survey*

The information in the chart on page 91 was put together by Statistics Canada. They get their information by asking lots of people questions. They then divide up the answers into categories such as province, age group, or male/female.

1. What basic question do you think Statistics Canada asked for this survey? _____

_____

2. Work with a small group to conduct your own TV survey. First, decide on the question you

will use. _____

3. Ask at least 20 people your question. Think about the answers you receive. You may want to ask follow-up questions.

4. Collect the results of your survey in a chart. Give your chart a title that indicates the topic of your survey.

EXTENDING: Divide up the result of your survey into categories: age group or male/female. Create a new chart to show the different categories or write a paragraph about your findings. Include a conclusion.

D WRITING *An Information Paragraph*

Follow these steps to write a short <u>information paragraph</u> about TV viewing in your province.

> An **information paragraph** is a paragraph that organizes facts or knowledge about a topic.

1. Circle the facts in the chart that include information about your province.

2. Use some of the following words or phrases as you write your paragraph:

on average	hours per week	total population	teens	Statistics Canada
viewing	average person	category	adults	children

3. Make a note, comparing TV viewing in your province with TV viewing in other provinces.
4. Write a concluding statement, perhaps explaining the survey results.

_____

_____

_____

_____

_____

_____

_____

_____

UNIT 4 WRAP-UP

 SELF-ASSESSMENT *Media*

1. Choose **one** topic below. In your notebook, explain what you learned about this topic as you worked on the *Media* unit.

   ❏ electronic communications technology
   ❏ how Canadian teenagers use the Internet
   ❏ Web safety
   ❏ testing TV shows
   ❏ how much TV Canadians watch

2. Think back to all the selections in this unit. In your notebook, describe the **three** most interesting facts you learned about the media. For each fact, explain how it has affected the way you think about media.

PROJECT IDEA *Survey*

Conduct a survey on a media issue or topic raised in this unit.

Step 1. With a partner, discuss the selections you read in this unit. Choose **one** of the following topics as a focus for your survey:

   ❏ favourite e-communications invention of the last 100 years
   ❏ most popular TV show
   ❏ time spent watching TV
   ❏ time spent on the computer
   ❏ Web safety
   ❏ movie-viewing habits
   ❏ a topic of your choice

Step 2. Think about what you would like to find out about people's opinions or behaviour related to this topic. Jot down the question or questions you plan to ask in your survey.

_____

_____

_____

Step 3. Plan how you will conduct your survey and how you will keep track of your results.
Step 4. Decide on the kind of chart or graph you will use to present your results. Make sure that you include good headings to show the type of information you have gathered.
Step 5. Write a paragraph analysing the results of your survey.

A **flowchart** clearly shows the order of a series of events. A flowchart helps you organize information and makes the information easier to understand.

IDENTIFY MAIN EVENTS OR STEPS

Begin by identifying the main events. Also identify any words that indicate when something happened or should happen (**first**, **last**, **during**, **ends**, **begins**, and so on). Highlight or underline that information in the text. ⎯⎯⎯⎯⎯⎯⎯⎯

> The movie, *All the Right Blood*, [10]ends in disaster: the hero, Alice, [8]dies just before her [9]world is destroyed. This horror movie begins with [1]Alice's birth. The audience sees her [2]grow up and [3]go to school. Alice has a happy, normal life. Until the day [4]aliens from Mars take over her hometown. [5]She organizes everyone in her community to fight the takeover, but [6]they can do nothing to save themselves. They are as helpless as ants before a lawnmower. There's some hope for the town, when [7]it looks like the aliens are retreating, but it's just a trap.

THINK ABOUT SEQUENCE

Next, think about the order in which these events have to happen. Number the events. Start with the first.

CREATE YOUR FLOWCHART

Organize the information into a flowchart that shows the order of the events or steps.

1. Alice is born.
↓
2. She grows up.
↓
3. She goes to school.
↓
4. Aliens take over her hometown.
↓
5. She organizes everyone to fight the aliens.
↓
6. The town can do nothing against the aliens.
↓
7. It looks like the aliens are retreating, but it's a trap.
↓
8. Alice dies.
↓
9. Her town is destroyed.
↓
10. The movie ends in disaster.

Before Reading
"The Human Body"

The next selection, "The Human Body," lists information about the following topics:

- ❏ the brain
- ❏ the five senses
- ❏ fitness activities
- ❏ what happens in the body during one day

A **KWL chart** (Know, Want to Know, Learned) can help you recall what you already know about a topic and help you think about new ideas and information. Use a KWL chart to record information and questions you have about the topics listed above.

KWL FOR THE HUMAN BODY

Topic	K What I KNOW	W What I WANT to Know	L What I LEARNED
The Brain			
The Five Senses			
Fitness Activities			
What Happens in the Body During One Day			

Using a KWL Chart

- In the **K** column, list **one** fact that you already **KNOW** for each of these topics.
- In the **W** column, list what you **WANT** to know about these topics. List at least **one** question for each topic.
- As you read "The Human Body," look for answers to your questions.
- **After** you have read the text, use the information you have **LEARNED** to write answers in the **L** column. If you have unanswered questions in the **W** column, think about where to find the answers.
- List any new questions you thought of as you read the text.

The Human Body

LISTS by Russell Ash

BRAIN FACTS

Heavy Head

An average brain weighs 1.3 kg.

Grey Matter

The **cortex** (outer layer of grey matter) of the brain is made up of nerve cell bodies. If the cortex were spread out flat, it would cover an office desk!

Cell Mates

One brain cell connects to about 25 000 others.

Left and Right

The brain is made up of two halves: the left controls logic and speech, and the right takes care of creativity.

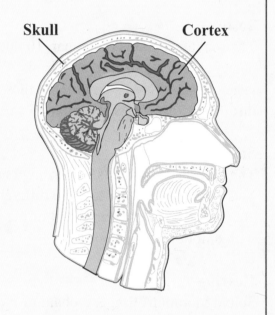

Skull   Cortex

IN ONE DAY...

✦ Your body sheds 36 million skin cells.
✦ Over 170 billion red blood cells are created and destroyed.
✦ Your heart beats 100 800 times.
✦ You take 30 000 breaths.
✦ Around 10 billion white blood cells are made.
✦ You blink 9365 times.
✦ Your kidneys filter 3600 L of blood. That's enough to fill 45 baths!
✦ You lose and replace 100 hairs.
✦ Enough body heat is produced to power a light bulb for 1.5 days.
✦ Your mouth produces 1 L of saliva.
✦ Your stomach produces 2 L of hydrochloric acid.
✦ About 5 mL of tears spills from your eyes. Crying empties out even more.

GOALS AT A GLANCE

elaborating on information • locating information

THE FIVE SENSES

Touch

The skin contains nerve endings that send messages to the brain and detect degrees of pressure, cold, warmth, and pain.

Taste

The tongue contains more than 10 000 taste buds that detect chemicals in food and drink. A baby is born with taste buds all over its mouth, but these taste buds slowly disappear. Taste buds are renewed weekly.

Smell

The nose detects smells by sensing chemicals in the air. You can identify 2000 to 4000 different smells. Smells are processed by the same part of the brain that deals with emotions and memories.

Hearing

Sound vibrations trigger a chain of movements in the skull. Our ears can detect 1500 different tones, 350 degrees of loudness, and can determine the direction of a sound within three degrees.

Sight

Light is detected by the eye and focused to form an image. Humans can detect a lighted candle 1.6 km away.

MOST EFFECTIVE FITNESS ACTIVITIES

These are the sports and activities recommended by fitness experts as the best means of acquiring all-around fitness, building stamina and strength, and increasing flexibility:

Swimming	Dancing	Cycling
Rowing	Jogging	Gymnastics
Judo	Soccer	Walking (briskly!)

A UNDERSTANDING THE SELECTION *Recalling Details*

Circle the <u>best</u> answer to complete each statement. When you have finished, check your answers against the information in the text.

1. The cortex
   a. is like a desk
   b. is made of nerve cell bodies
   c. is the inner layer of the brain
   d. controls logic and speech

2. Activities recommended by many fitness experts include
   a. dancing   **b.** walking briskly   **c.** cycling   **d.** all of the above

3. The average person has more than
   a. 1000 taste buds   **b.** 10 000 taste buds   **c.** 100 000 taste buds   **d.** 2000 taste buds

4. You detect smells because your nose senses
   a. emotions and memories
   b. chemicals in the air
   c. 2000 different smells
   d. your brain

5. In one day, your body gets rid of
   a. skin cells   **b.** tears   **c.** hair   **d.** all of the above   **e.** none of the above

B CRITICAL THINKING *Elaborating on Information*

1. Why do you think taste buds in the mouth are renewed weekly? _____

   _____

2. How does our sense of touch protect us? _____

   _____

3. Describe one situation when a strong smell sparked a certain memory for you. _____

   _____

   _____

4. Choose **one** of the sports and activities in the "Most Effective Fitness Activities" box.
   Explain why you think it was included.

   _____

   _____

   _____

   _____

C RESEARCHING *Locating Information*

1. Choose one topic from "The Human Body" that you want to learn more about.
2. What do you already know about the topic? What questions do you have?
   Start a KWL chart for that topic.
3. Research to find answers to your questions. The tips below will be useful if
   you're using the Internet for your research.
4. Complete the KWL chart.

EXTENDING: Use the information you find to create an information box like the ones in
"The Human Body." Organize your facts in an easy-to-read format such as a chart,
a labelled diagram, or a list. Give your information box a title.

Locating Information on the Internet

- Use a search engine such as Google, AltaVista, or Yahoo.
- Choose an appropriate search word or phrase. For example, if you want to
  find information on the heart, type in **human heart**. If you use quotation
  marks around search words ("human heart"), your search engine will look
  for that exact phrase.
- Scan the titles on the list that appears. Click on any titles that seem useful.
- Check the author or source of the information. Does it seem reliable?
- Print up any pages you want to look at. Highlight important information.

D LANGUAGE CONVENTIONS *Conjunctions*

- A **conjunction** is a word used to join words, groups of words, or sentences.
- To add variety to your writing, you can join two complete sentences using the
  conjunctions <u>and</u>, <u>but</u>, <u>or</u>. This makes a **compound sentence**. In compound sentences,
  a comma comes before the conjunction.
  EXAMPLE: A baby is born with taste buds all over its mouth<u>, but</u> these taste buds
  slowly disappear.

<u>Underline</u> **the conjunction in each sentence and add a comma. Each sentence needs one
comma.**

1. An average brain weighs 1.3 kg and its cortex is made of nerve cell bodies.

2. Every day your body sheds 36 million skin cells but only 100 hairs are lost during that time.

3. The left brain controls logic and the right brain handles creativity.

4. Heart disease is the most common cause of death worldwide but cancer is not far behind.

Before Reading

Do you read about a product before you buy it? _____

Skim the text below. Think about how this information can help you shop for a backpack.

A Better Backpack for Your Back

ONLINE ARTICLE from *Zillions® Magazine, Consumer Reports® for Kids*

Another year of school has almost passed. How's your back holding up? Doctors are seeing more and more kids with back pain caused by backpacks. Can anything help kids' aching backs? Here's some information to help ease backpack pain.

BACK-FRIENDLY FEATURES

Good backpacks have
- two shoulder straps
- back support
- side and chest straps
- a waist belt
- padded straps and back

Here's what back-friendly features like these can do.

1. Distribute weight evenly across your back.
The more spread out a load is, the less strain it puts on any one part of your body.

2. Keep the load close to your body.
The further a backpack's load is from your back, the more it pulls you backward and strains muscles between your shoulders. Keeping the pack close to your hips also shifts "work" to your legs.

3. Absorb force.
Padding keeps straps from digging into and pinching shoulders. Padded backs keep heavy loads from poking your back.

GOALS AT A GLANCE

identifying sources • writing an information paragraph

BACK-FRIENDLY BACKPACK CHECKLIST

This backpack is jammed with features that can help lessen the strain on your back.

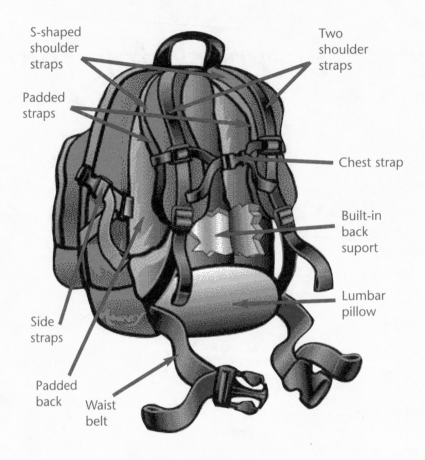

S-shaped shoulder straps

Padded straps

Two shoulder straps

Chest strap

Built-in back suport

Lumbar pillow

Side straps

Padded back

Waist belt

HOW TO WEAR A BACKPACK

Wearing a backpack properly can prevent back pain. Here are some tips:

- Wear both shoulder straps.
- Use the waist belt.
- Use the side/chest straps.
- Position the backpack so that the bottom rests in the curve of your lower back and the top touches just below the big knob on your neck.
- Tighten the shoulder straps so the pack fits close to the upper part of your back.
- Load the backpack so that the heaviest items are right next to your back.
- Don't load too much into your backback. You should be able to lift it easily.

BACKPACK SURVEY

Complete this survey. Compare your answers with other classmates. What conclusions can you draw from the results of this survey?

1. What do you carry schoolbooks and other stuff in when going to and from school?

   - ❏ Backpack
   - ❏ Wheeled luggage/rolling backpack
   - ❏ Sports bag
   - ❏ Other
   - ❏ Carry loose

2. If you use a backpack or bag, how many shoulder straps does it have?

   - ❏ Two
   - ❏ One

3. If you use a backpack or bag, how do you usually carry it?

   - ❏ On both shoulders
   - ❏ On one shoulder
   - ❏ Other

4. How heavy is the stuff you carry to and from school?

   - ❏ Very heavy
   - ❏ Heavy
   - ❏ Not too bad
   - ❏ Light
   - ❏ Very light

5. Do you ever get backache?

   - ❏ Never
   - ❏ Sometimes
   - ❏ Often

1. Complete the following webs using information from the article and its diagrams. You can use point form.

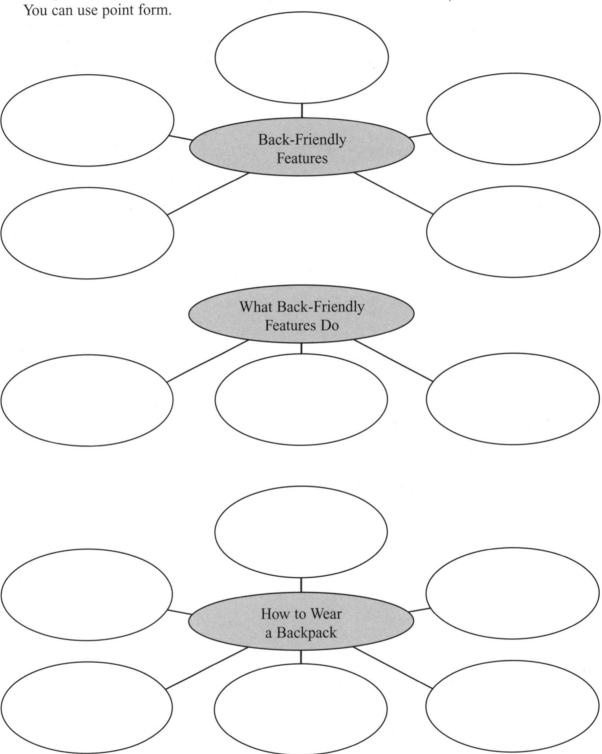

Back-Friendly Features

What Back-Friendly Features Do

How to Wear a Backpack

2. Look over your webs. Explain to a partner how creating the webs helped increase your understanding of the article.

1. Use the following Venn diagram to compare the features of your backpack (or a friend's) with the labelled backpack in the article.

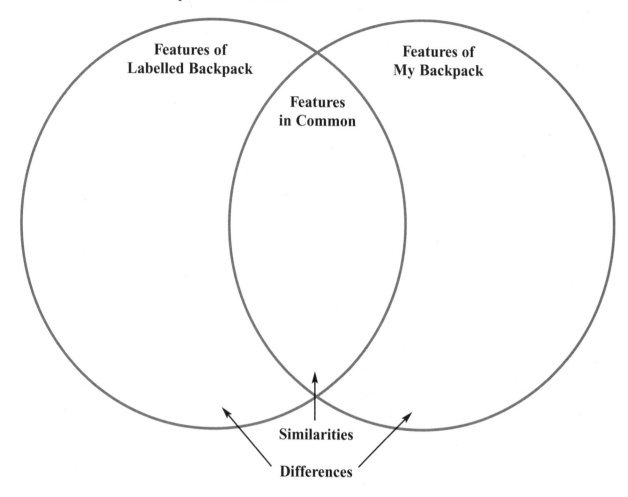

Features of
Labelled Backpack

Features of
My Backpack

Features
in Common

Similarities

Differences

2. Look at all the features you have listed where the two circles intersect. How does your backpack measure up?

_____

_____

_____

Using a Venn Diagram

A Venn diagram can help you compare and contrast two things, events, ideas, or people.
- Each thing being compared has its own circle.
- The similarities between the things go in the space where the two circles overlap.
- Write the differences in the other part of each circle.

What product do you want to buy? (For example, a video game, a bike, puppy, backpack, or jeans.) Research to get consumer information about this product.

1. Visit the library. Ask the librarian to help you find magazines to help you with your purchase. What magazines did you find helpful? _____

2. Use the library's computer or card catalogue to look for books about your product.

   What titles did you find? _____

   _____

3. Use the Internet and choose a search engine (see page 100 for some tips) to search for information on the product.

   a. What search words did you use? _____

   b. What **three** sites did you find most helpful?_____

   _____

4. Ask experts (people who use it or make it) about your product.

   a. What experts did you ask? _____

   b. What questions did you ask? _____

   _____

D   **WRITING** *Information Paragraph*

Use the information you gathered in activity C to write an information paragraph on the product.

Information Paragraph

A good information paragraph includes the following:
- a **topic sentence** that clearly states what the paragraph is about
- **supporting details** that back-up your topic sentence; these can be facts you've learned in your research or personal examples or experiences
- a **conclusion** that sums up the information you gathered in your research

1. Begin with a **topic sentence**.
2. Your paragraph should include some of the information you learned as you researched the product. Include **supporting details** for some of the points.
3. Write a **conclusion** to your information paragraph.

Before Reading
"Chills, Thrills, and Spills"

The magazine article "Chills, Thrills, and Spills" is about thrill rides at amusement parks. With a small group, **brainstorm** answers to these questions:

- Why do so many people like thrill rides?
- Why do some people hate thrill rides?

When you are finished, get together with another group and share your answers.

> When you **brainstorm**, the whole group contributes all their ideas on one topic. Write down every idea. Listen as well as talk, because other people's comments will trigger ideas.

Listening

- Pay attention when others are speaking.
- If you don't understand what someone has said, ask the person to explain.
- Don't interrupt when others are speaking. Jot down a note to remind you of what you want to say and then speak when the other person is finished.

During Reading

Step 1. Fill in the second column of this vocabulary chart completely. Now, fill in as much of the rest of the chart as you can.

Step 2. While you are reading the article, look for these vocabulary words. Underline them. If you can, fill in other spaces on the chart.

VOCABULARY CHART

Words	Have I Seen or Heard This Word Before?	This Word Means	Sample Sentence Using the Word
queasy			
plunges			
warp speed			
virtual			

Chills, Thrills, and Spills

MAGAZINE ARTICLE by Samantha Bonar from *Owl* Magazine

ROCKET TO THE TOP

It seems like you had to stand in that lineup forever, but now you're finally seated. Your car slowly begins to inch up the tower.

"This is kind of nice," you think.

Suddenly, you are **smooshed** into your seat as your car rockets straight to the top of a 90-m high tower in three seconds flat. You start to feel a little queasy when your car pauses at the top of the tower, but you take a deep breath and feel a bit better. OK, you're cool. This isn't so bad... AHHHH!

Without warning, your car plunges back to Earth at what seems like warp speed. It stops just seconds before it hits the ground. Phew! You've just experienced the Power Tower, the newest thrill ride at Cedar Point amusement park in Sandusky, Ohio. Do you want to ride it again? And again and again?

I WANT TO GET OFF!

Why are thrill rides like the Power Tower so popular when they're such a terrifying experience?

Well, sometimes scaring yourself silly can make you feel good! When you're scared, your body releases a substance called **adrenalin** into your blood. Adrenalin makes your palms sweaty, your pupils open wide, and your heart race. It also makes you feel excited.

Some people like this "adrenalin rush" so much that they try out activities like skydiving to get their adrenalin pumping. Other people just feel sick and scared with an adrenalin rush, and would never think of skydiving or even going on a roller coaster.

GOALS AT A GLANCE

assessing strategies • thinking about audience and tone

THAT'S SICK!

So why do you sometimes feel dizzy and sick when you step off a ride? It's called **motion sickness** and it happens because your brain is getting different messages about which way is up.

Your inner ears, which help manage body balance, send signals to your brain that scream: "We're upside down!" But by the time your brain receives that message, it gets another one from your eyes: "We're right-side up!" The position of your body is changing so fast that your brain can't keep up. So it gets confused and you feel dizzy.

Some scientists believe all this confusion may also make your brain think you're being poisoned. So your body decides to get that "poison" out of you and (you guessed it!) you throw up!

Visitors to Thorpe Park in England ride the Colossus, a ten-loop roller coaster that goes up to 65 k/h on 850 m of twisting track.

THE FORCE IS WITH YOU

When you're hurtling along on a ride, you are probably too busy trying to keep your lunch down to notice that there are forces at work on you.

Force is a push or pull against something. (For example, gravity is a force that pulls objects toward the Earth.) Some types of force are measured in units called **g's**. You always have one g of gravity pulling you to the ground. But you're so used to it that you don't feel it. When you speed up a hill on a coaster, though, you're pushing against gravity. So you have more g's (up to 4) of force pulling on you. That's why you feel squished!

Then once you go over the hill, the car goes down and your body keeps going up. For a second, no g's are pulling on you, so it may feel like you're floating. Eeek!

VIRTUALLY THRILLING

Some of the world's most exciting rides don't even go one kilometre per hour! Huh? They're called **virtual reality rides**, and they use special effects to make you feel like you're moving even though you're not. In fact, you can "experience" anything from hang-gliding to a river-rafting trip among dinosaurs, while staying in your seat the entire time!

These rides work by getting your eyes to fool your brain. You see, your brain gets most of its information about what's going on around you from your eyes. So these rides use visual tricks to make it **look** like you're moving along with whatever is onscreen, and your brain decides that you must **really** be moving.

Most virtual rides take place in a theatre with a huge screen, a loud sound system, and chairs that move to match the onscreen action. Instead of a screen, you may wear goggles that show computer images. In both cases, the rides are so realistic that some people get sick to their stomachs!

Riders on the Dopple Looping roller coaster go through a loop on the first day of the Canadian National Exhibition in Toronto.

A READING *Assessing Strategies*

1. Return to the brainstorming notes your group made before reading the article. Highlight notes that gave information that also appeared in the text.
2. Check that you have completely filled in the vocabulary chart on page 107. Create a similar chart for **three** other difficult words in the selection.

Reflecting

3. **a.** How did your brainstorming session prepare you for reading the article?

   _____

   _____

   b. How did completing the vocabulary chart help prepare you for reading the article?

   _____

   _____

B UNDERSTANDING THE SELECTION *Organizing Information*

1. Complete the second column of this chart using information from the magazine article. You can use point form.
2. Complete the third column by describing a personal experience you've had that connects with each question and answer.

Question	Answer	Personal Connection
Why do some people enjoy going on thrill rides?		
Why do some people hate thrill rides?		
How does gravity help put the **thrill** in thrill ride?		
How does a virtual reality ride work?		

C CRITICAL THINKING *Thinking About Audience and Tone*

1. The writer of the magazine article, Samantha Bonar, has used the following style elements. Circle **two** examples of each element in the article. In the margin, label your examples, using the code in **bold** CAPITALS before each point.

   Q   - questions to the reader
   CON - conversation
   SL   - informal language or slang (cool, wow, guts)
   VV   - strong or vivid description (That incredible ride made me splash my guts.)
   YOU - speaking directly to the reader (using your/you)

2. **a.** Do you think the writer wrote this article for adults or young people? _____
   b. Explain your answer using the examples you circled.

   _____

   _____

   _____

3. Circle **three** other sentences or phrases in the article that you think appeal to this audience. Explain why you think so.

   _____

   _____

   _____

D VISUAL COMMUNICATION *Design a Thrill Ride*

Imagine you've been given the job of designing a new thrill ride for an amusement park in your community. Follow these instructions to design the thrill ride.

1. Think about the features of thrill rides listed in the article.
2. Think about some of the thrill rides you've enjoyed. Why did you enjoy them?
3. List all the features you want to include on your thrill ride.

```



```

4. Draw a diagram or picture of your thrill ride. Label all the features you've included.

EXTENDING: Use craft or found materials to create a model of your thrill ride.

- An **adjective** is a word that describes a noun or pronoun. Adjectives usually tell **which one**, **what kind**, or **how many**.

  EXAMPLES: newest, queasy, dizzy, realistic, this, nine

- When you are writing, choose vivid, descriptive adjectives that make the scene or experience come alive for the reader.

  BEFORE: It was a <u>scary</u> experience.

  AFTER: It was a <u>terrifying</u> experience.

---

1. <u>Underline</u> the adjectives in the following sentences. Circle the noun or pronoun that each adjective describes.

   a. I was excited about riding the new roller coaster.

   b. A large man screamed that he wanted off the ride.

   c. His son loved the wild ride and wanted to go again.

2. Think about a thrill ride you have experienced. Complete the following word web using vivid, descriptive adjectives.

Words to Describe the Ride	——	Thrill Ride	——	Words to Describe the Experience

3. Write a descriptive paragraph about the thrill ride. Use at least **ten** of the vivid adjectives you listed in your word web.

4. Think about how making a list of adjectives helped you to write your descriptive paragraph. How might this strategy help you with other writing?

_____

_____

_____

Before Reading

Read the title below. Make a prediction about the topic of this article.

_____

_____

Skim the article reading the headings for each section and looking at the picture.
Is your prediction about the topic the same or different? Explain why.

_____

_____

_____

Life in a Bubble

SCIENCE ARTICLE AND EXPERIMENT from *The Book of You* by Sylvia Funston

You're in a crowded elevator. What do you do?
If you're like most people, you face the door.
Then, with a blank look on your face, you study the
flashing floor numbers as if they hold the secret of life.
What is it about you and your fellow passengers that
makes you act so weird?

Here are some clues. Everyone has it, even babies.
As you grow, it grows. It takes up more space in front of
you than behind. And it shrinks when you're with people
you trust. Got it yet? It's your **personal space**. Think of
it as an invisible force field with you at its centre or like
a space bubble; when people get too close, it bursts!

GOALS AT A GLANCE

completing a summary • conducting an interview

TOO CLOSE FOR COMFORT

Most people don't intrude into other people's space bubbles unless invited. But sometimes, like in crowded elevators or on rush-hour trains and buses, we're forced to be uncomfortably close. Then we shrink our space bubbles, and avoid feeling threatened by pretending other people don't exist. We don't make eye contact or let our faces show that we know they're there.

Your space bubble gives you a small territory over which you're boss. By learning how and when to give up some of your space, you co-operate with others and <u>defuse</u> stressful situations without having to use your fists!

HOW BIG IS YOUR SPACE BUBBLE?

You're about to measure the size of your personal space. How big do you think it will be? Record your prediction here. _____

People who live or work together often include favourite objects in their personal space. For instance, does your home have a "Dad" or a "Mom" chair that no one else sits in? Do you all have your own places around the table?

You'll need:
- some friends
- a tape measure
- pencil and paper

1. Ask a friend to stand 2 m away from you. (Measure nose to nose.)

2. Have your friend look only at your chin. With arms by his or her side and no facial expression, your friend walks slowly toward you. Look at your friend's eyes.

3. Say "stop" the moment you feel your friend is too close.

4. Measure and record your space bubble distance, nose to nose.

5. Repeat with other friends.

6. To find your **average** space bubble distance with friends, add up all the space bubble distances and divide the total by the number of friends. For example, your equation might look like this for 5 friends:

   (10 cm + 16 cm + 12 cm + 18 cm + 14 cm) ÷ 5 = 14

   So 14 cm would be your average space bubble distance.

7. Repeat the experiment with your best friend and your family. Is there a difference in the results?

   Were you surprised by the results of this experiment? Explain.

   _____

   _____

   _____

Space at Your Fingertips

Next time you're talking to someone you know, and you're comfortable with the distance between you, raise your arm. Is the space between you the full length of your arm (shoulder to fingertips), from shoulder to wrist, or shoulder to elbow?

A UNDERSTANDING THE SELECTION *Completing a Summary*

Complete this summary of "Life in a Bubble."

When you are in a crowded space, such as an _____ ,

you may feel uncomfortably _____ to other people. This

is because other people are in your _____ .

Many people respond to this situation by pretending that the people around them don't

_____ .

Personal space is like an _____ force field or space

_____ . It is the space you like to keep between yourself

and other _____ .

Personal space is a small _____ where

you are boss. However, in crowded places you need to _____

with others and _____ some of that space.

B VISUAL COMMUNICATION *Thinking About Design Features*

1. a. What did you notice first when you looked at the article?

_____

b. What made this item or feature stand out?

_____

2. Explain how the photo on page 115 illustrates the information in the rest of the text.

_____

3. Why do you think the experiment "How Big Is Your Space Bubble?" was written in numbered steps instead of as a paragraph?

_____

_____

C ORAL COMMUNICATION *Conducting an Interview*

1. Make up **three** interview questions to ask a classmate, friend, or family member about issues raised in the text. You might ask about:

   - their own sense of personal space
   - situations in which their personal space is invaded
   - their reactions to such situations

   _____

   _____

   _____

2. Record the answers you get to your questions.

   _____

   _____

   _____

   _____

EXTENDING: Meet with a group of classmates. Share your answers and discuss the similarities and differences you found. Explain why you think any answers are different.

D LANGUAGE CONVENTIONS *Adverbs*

> - An **adverb** is a word that describes a verb, an adjective, or another adverb.
>   EXAMPLES: happily, uncomfortably, closely, well, slowly, too, very, there.
>
> - Adverbs usually tell **how**, **when**, **where**, or **how often**.
> - Many adverbs end in **-ly**.

1. Underline the adverbs in the following sentences.

   a. Suddenly, we were flying. _____

   b. Sandra runs faster than you do. _____

   c. Jason always rides his bike. _____

   d. Everywhere you go, you'll find people are the same. _____

   e. That store is open late. _____

2. In the blank space, indicate whether the above adverbs tell **how**, **when**, **where**, or **how often**.

Before Reading

Do you always trust your eyes or do they sometimes play tricks on you? Take a look at these optical illusions and see what you can see. Then read the explanations and notes for these tricks on page 122.

THE ART OF OPTICAL ILLUSIONS

OPTICAL ILLUSIONS collected by Al Seckel

1. SHEPARD'S TABLETOP

The two tabletops are absolutely identical in size and shape! If you don't believe it, trace only the tabletops and see for yourself.

GOALS AT A GLANCE

explaining the illusion • reporting

2. FLOATING FINGER ILLUSION

You can make a finger float right before your eyes in this fun illusion. Hold both of your hands in front of your face at eye level. Keep the tips of your index fingers also at eye level. Focus on a wall several feet behind your fingers. You should see a finger float. Try moving your fingers closer to your face. What happens? If you focus on your fingers, instead of the wall, the illusion vanishes.

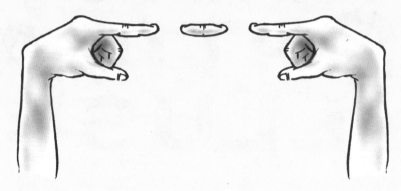

3. TWISTED CIRCLES

This is a series of perfect **concentric** [having the same centre] circles! This is an example of a twisted cord illusion.

4. DUCK/RABBIT

What do you see, a rabbit or a duck?

5. ILLUSORY MOVEMENT

Shake this image and you will see **illusory** [false, not real] movement.

EXPLANATIONS AND NOTES

1. Shepard's Tabletop

Although the drawing is flat, it suggests a **three-dimensional** (three-D) object. The table's edges and legs provide perspective cues that influence your **interpretation** [understanding] of its three-D shape. This powerful illusion clearly demonstrates that your brain does not take a **literal** [exact or truthful] interpretation of what it sees. Stanford psychologist Roger Shepard created this illusion

2. Floating Finger Illusion

By focusing on the wall, the two fingers in the foreground incorrectly overlap when the images from both eyes are automatically combined. These overlapping images produce a **stereogram** [solid or three-D image] with the floating finger.

3. Twisted Circles

The "twisted cord" that forms the concentric circles creates the illusion of a spiral. Look at the centre spot. Do you get the impression that you're falling into a hole or looking through a tube?

4. Duck/Rabbit

Both interpretations are possible in this classic illusion. Many left-handed people see the rabbit before the duck, and many right-handed people see the duck before the rabbit. What did you see first? This illusion was created by psychologist Joseph Jastrow around 1900.

5. Illusory Movement

Try to focus on one point in this illusion. Do the dots seem to grow in size? Does the illusion make your eyes cross? Watch out, staring at this illusion for too long may give you a headache.

UNDERSTANDING THE SELECTION *Explaining the Illusion*

1. Choose **one** of the optical illusions in the selection. Read the information for that illusion on page 122.
2. In your own words, explain how the illusion works or what happens when you look at it.

_____

_____

_____

_____

_____

_____

3. Share your explanation with a partner. Does your partner understand your explanation? How could you change your explanation to make it clearer?

_____

_____

_____

_____

_____

B CRITICAL THINKING *Personal Response*

Answer the following questions in your notebook.

1. Which optical illusion in the selection did you like best? Why?
2. What do you like (or dislike) about optical illusions?
3. Do you like to know how optical illusions work? Why or why not?
4. Why do you think so many people enjoy viewing optical illusions?

EXTENDING: Use your answers to write an information paragraph on optical illusions.

C RESEARCHING *Oral Report*

1. Go to your local library or use the Internet to find other optical illusions.
2. Choose an optical illusion that you think is really clever.
3. Write a short note explaining how the illusion works or what happens when you look at it.
4. Share this illusion and your explanation with your class.

UNIT 5 WRAP-UP

SELF-ASSESSMENT *Using Graphic Organizers*

1. Check off each of the following graphic organizers that you read or used in this unit:

   ❏ list
   ❏ KWL chart
   ❏ idea or word web
   ❏ Venn diagram
   ❏ diagrams
   ❏ vocabulary chart
   ❏ Question/Answer/Personal Connection chart

2. Choose **one** graphic organizer listed above. In your notebook, describe the strategies you used to help you read or use that graphic organizer.

PROJECT IDEA *Research Report*

Follow these steps to research and write a report on a topic connected to this unit.

Step 1. Think about the topics you read about in the *Body Science* unit. Choose **one** topic that you want to research. Create a web like this one to help you generate topic ideas.

Step 2. Create a KWL chart for your topic. Include at least **four** questions in the **W** column.

Step 3. Research your questions. Use the researching tips on page 100 to help you. When you find answers to your questions, fill in the **L** column of the chart.

Step 4. Highlight the information in the KWL chart that you will include in your report. If you have printed pages from the Internet with important information, highlight information on those pages too.

Step 5. Create an outline for your research report. An outline should indicate the main topic of your report and the topic of each paragraph.

Step 6. Write a report with at least **three** information paragraphs. Include at least **one** of the following:

   ❏ diagram   ❏ list
   ❏ photo or picture ❏ experiment
   ❏ Venn diagram   ❏ instructions
   ❏ idea web   ❏ survey

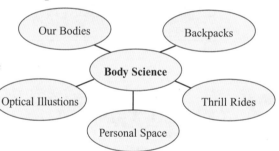

A <u>Venn diagram</u> can help you compare and contrast two things, events, ideas, or people. You can use a Venn diagram after you research to help you organize your ideas on a topic. A Venn diagram can also help you or your audience see how two things are related.

Step 1. In a Venn diagram, each thing being compared has its own circle. These circles overlap.

For example, if you wanted to contrast and compare thrill rides and virtual reality rides, you would start with a Venn diagram that looks like this:

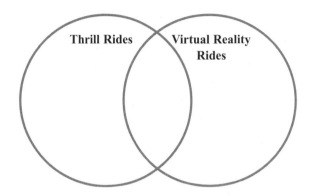

Step 2. List the **similarities** between the things in the space where the two circles overlap.

This is what the Venn diagram comparing thrill rides and virtual reality rides would look like at this stage.

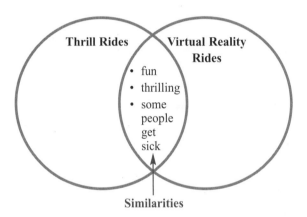

Step 3. List the **differences** in the other part of each circle. Before you list each point, think carefully about where it belongs. Sometimes, when you think about a difference again, you may realize it's actually a similarity.

This is what the final Venn diagram comparing thrill rides and virtual reality rides would look like.

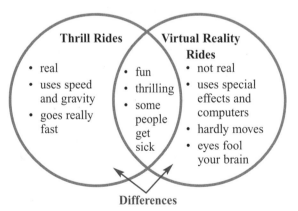

Step 4. When your Venn diagram is complete, look it over. Think about how you have organized your information. Think about the relationships you can see between the two topics.

Before Reading

Can you remember a time you felt unwanted? How did it make you feel?

_____

_____

_____

On November 14, 1960, in New Orleans, Louisiana, Ruby Bridges became the first black child to attend a school where previously only white students had been allowed. This was a time of great civil unrest in the southern United States. Many black people were fighting for equal rights and an end to **segregation** (laws that separated white and black people in schools and other public places).

In this personal narrative, William Joyce tells about a personal experience he had during that time.

A Small Victory

PERSONAL NARRATIVE by William Joyce
from _Tikvah: Children's Book Creators Reflect on Human Rights_

> VOCABULARY
>
> **integration**: a program to include black and white students in the same schools
>
> **in earnest**: seriously

Integration of the public schools in Louisiana began in earnest the year I started junior high school. I was 13 years old and these would be the first black kids I had ever met.

All the grown-ups were very tense. Parents. Newscasters. Newspaper reporters. Police. Teachers. Ministers. Everybody over five feet tall [about 150 cm] and of voting age looked ready for the end of the world.

The big day came. The grown-up world held its breath…and nothing happened. Or at least nothing they expected. A bunch of kids just went to school. They got along. They learned together. They played together. Everything was cool.

> GOALS AT A GLANCE
>
> making inferences • writing personal narrative

Haven Small, a fellow 13-year-old, fell into our group as naturally and as easily as a breeze. His colour had no more place in our thoughts than if he'd had freckles. He came home with me one day. My parents were very nice, but after Haven left they told me that a black kid was not welcome in our house. Not now. Not ever.

I felt something inside I still cannot put into words. I told them I was embarrassed by them. I'd thought they weren't like that. I'd thought they were better than that. There was a long afternoon of quiet in our house. At dinner they apologized. They told me that from now on Haven, or any other friend of mine, was welcome in our home. Times had changed and they would change with them, they said.

Whatever failings my parents had, they had taught me to stand up for what I thought was right and they had listened on the rare times I had complaints. Their giving in so calmly, however, surprised even me. I guess it really was time for things to change.

After school, a few days later, our group drifted to the house of another classmate. Her father greeted us at the door and ordered us to leave. His daughter was not allowed to have boys over. His tone was stern, unkind, almost hateful. We wandered away. We knew the real reason why he made us leave. Even worse, Haven knew why too. I'll never forget the look on Haven's face. Wounded and <u>humiliated</u>, he had a sadness I could witness but never fully understand. Things like that didn't happen to white kids.

VOCABULARY

bigotry: hating others without even knowing them, because they are different

blight: something that destroys

At my home a small victory had been won. Down the street a bitter enemy of equality and kindness had held his ground. I don't know if <u>bigotry</u> will ever completely disappear, but every small victory chips away at this <u>blight</u> on our better natures. Someday, with luck and continuing effort, no 13-year-old will ever be made to feel that low again.

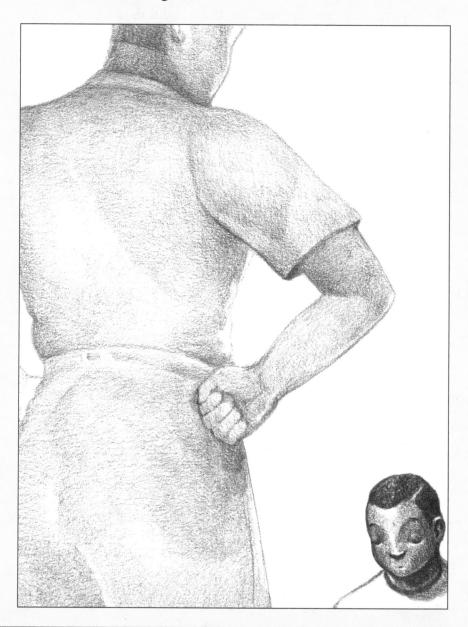

Author/Illustrator Profile

William Joyce is a children's book author and illustrator. He has created over a dozen classics, including *George Shrinks* (now a TV show), *Buddy*, *Baseball Bob*, and *Rolie Polie Olie*. William wrote his first book when he was in Grade 2, and says that being raised by a kindly "horde of southern screwballs" has made writing and illustrating easy for him.

Viewing an Image

- Identify the **subject** of the picture. Ask yourself: What is happening here?
- Think about the **design** of the picture (colours, shapes, or lines).
- Think about the **feelings** or **ideas** the artist is trying to communicate.

1. Beside the picture on page 128, write the following:
   - **one** comment about the subject of the picture
   - **one** comment about the design of the picture
   - **one** comment about the feelings the picture communicates
   - **one** comment about the ideas the picture communicates
2. Read over your comments. Write **one** statement that summarizes all your comments.

B   UNDERSTANDING THE SELECTION *Identifying Main Events*

1. Turn back to pages 126 to 128. In the margin, write the following headings where you think they belong:

   Integration in Louisiana Schools
   Haven Small Starts School
   A Time for Things to Change
   Not Everyone Accepts Change
   Will Bigotry Ever Disappear?

2. Reread each section you have identified with a heading. Write a short statement explaining more fully what happened in that section or identifying the main idea. You can write your statements in the margin.

3. Did you find that this activity increased your understanding of the selection?

   Explain your answer. _____

   _____

Try using this strategy as you read another text: divide the text into sections, give each section a heading, and write a statement about the section.

Identifying Main Events

Identifying the main events (or ideas) of a text is an important step in understanding it.

- Reread any parts you don't understand. If you still don't understand, discuss those parts with a classmate or your teacher.
- Highlight important information in each section.
- Divide the text into sections, using headings that make sense.
- Write down one statement to explain what is happening in each section.
- Think about how your headings and statements reflect the text.

C CRITICAL THINKING *Making Inferences*

1. Why do you think the adults and the children react differently to the integration of the schools? _____

_____

2. What did the father mean when he said his daughter was "not allowed to have boys over"?

_____

_____

3. Why do you think the author remembers this experience so clearly?

_____

_____

_____

EXTENDING: Have you ever experienced prejudice because of your appearance, cultural heritage, or religion? Explain.

D VOCABULARY *Using Root Words to Work Out Meaning*

- A **root** is a word or part of a word that can be used to form other words.
  EXAMPLE: <u>equal</u> <u>equal</u>ity un<u>equal</u> <u>equal</u>ize
  root

- When you read an unfamiliar word, see if you can find a root word in it. If you know the meaning of the root word, you may be able to figure out the meaning of the whole word. For example, William Joyce uses the word **failings**. You may recognize that the first part of this word is **fail**, and you know that **fail** means "not able to do something."

1. <u>Underline</u> the root word of each word below.

   a. unkind **b.** hateful   **c.** kindness   **d.** disappear   **e.** victory

2. Form **one** or more new words using the following root words.

   a. expect _____   **b.** report _____

   c. allow _____   **d.** sad _____

   e. understand _____   **f.** news _____

E WRITING *A Personal Narrative*

1. Read the characteristics of a personal narrative in the following checklist. Check off each characteristic that you think "A Small Victory" has.

   ❏ A **personal narrative** describes an important event in a writer's life.

   ❏ The writer tells **who** was involved, **what** happened, **where** and **when** it happened, and explains **why** or **how** things happened as they did.

   ❏ The writing is organized in **time order** (in the order it happened). Words such as **once**, **later**, **soon**, **during**, or **finally** are used.

   ❏ The writer's **feelings** (angry, hopeful, happy) about the event are reflected in the tone of the writing.

   ❏ The writer ends by reflecting on the **importance** of the event

2. Use the planner below to help you write a personal narrative for an important event in your own life.

Personal Narrative Planner
What is the important event?
Who is involved? (Name and describe each person.)
What happened? (Use time order to list everything that happened.)
Where and when is your story taking place?
Why or how did this event happen?
How did this event make you feel?
Why is this event important? What can others learn by reading your story?

3. Write your personal narrative. It should be at least **one** page long.
4. Use the checklist at the top of the page. Check that you have included each characteristic of a personal narrative.
5. Give your personal narrative a good title. Add an illustration.

Before Reading

"The 'Man in the Family' Is Just a Boy"

In 1996, the Taliban gained control of the government of Afghanistan. The Taliban allowed al-Qaeda, a terrorist organization, to set up training bases in Afghanistan. After the terrorist attacks of September 11, 2001, the United States, Canada, and other countries sent troops to Afghanistan. This is a newspaper article about an Afghan boy injured during the war.

Developing Understanding

- As you read the article, highlight anything you don't understand.
- When you finish reading, go back over the parts you highlighted. Check if you now have the information you need to figure out those parts.
- Discuss any parts you are still unsure about with a partner or a small group.

VOCABULARY

breadwinner: the member of a family who earns all or most of the money for food and shelter

Uzbek: one of the languages spoken in Afghanistan

interpreter: person who translates from one language to another

UNICEF: United Nations Children's Fund

perched: seated on something high

stirrups: part of the saddle where you put your feet

shrapnel: pieces of an exploded bomb

Northern Alliance: rebel forces fighting against the Taliban government

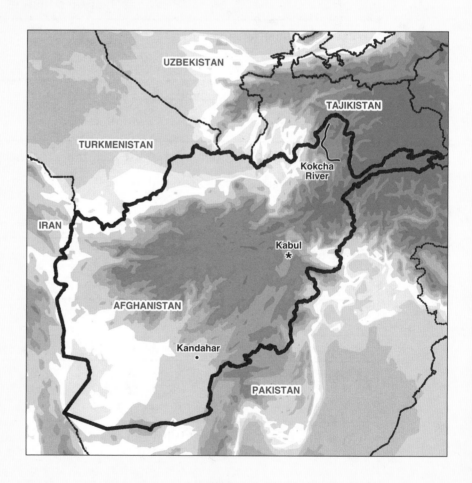

The "Man in the Family" Is Just a Boy

NEWSPAPER ARTICLE by Alan Freeman
The Globe and Mail, November 8, 2001

Abdulawal may be no older than ten but already he's the <u>breadwinner</u> for his family. Seven days a week, Abdulawal takes his dark brown horse to the shores of the Kokcha River. There he waits with other horsemen who take passengers across the swift-flowing river near Afghanistan's northern border with Tajikistan.

Six years ago his father, a soldier in the Afghan army, died. As the eldest of four boys, Abdulawal became responsible for his family's fate.

"There was nobody else to work in the family. I am now the man in the family," he says in <u>Uzbek</u>, speaking through an <u>interpreter</u>.

Ask Yourself
What do you think Abdulawal's biggest challenge is?

A beautiful child with a ready grin, Abdulawal looks as if he should spend his days playing, or at least learning to read and write. But this is Afghanistan, where most of the population can't read or write. A <u>UNICEF</u> report says 90% of girls and more than 65% of boys are not enrolled in school.

Many children work to put rice and beans on the table. They lead donkeys, bash metal, chop wood, or are horsemen, like Abdulawal.

GOALS AT A GLANCE

synthesizing • writing an e-mail message

"I work every day," he says, _perched_ atop a saddle fashioned from blankets and leather and stuffed with straw. Without _stirrups_, he has to depend on the strength of his small legs and bare feet to keep him on his horse.

"It's not regular work. Sometimes I cross five times a day, sometimes ten."

Business is particularly good these days for the horsemen. Foreign journalists pay $20 (U.S.) for a return trip across the river, the only way to get to the nearby Taliban front lines.

What is unusual about Abdulawal is that he manages his job despite the disaster that happened earlier this year. While playing on the shore of the river with his brother, a Taliban shell landed nearby. _Shrapnel_ smashed his shoulder and hit his chest.

"I went to hospital and stayed there for six days." Though he is back at work, he can no longer lift his right arm properly or pick up anything heavy. "When it's cold, it becomes worse. I still have pain in my shoulder."

It is unclear how much money Abdulawal keeps for himself and how much he has to pay to the local _Northern Alliance_ commander.

His profits, after paying for feed and shoes for his horse, go to his mother. He says, though, that he keeps some for candy and for clothing, pointing to a pair of what are clearly homemade trousers that have been mended many times. As for his future, Abdulawal seems puzzled when he is asked what he will do when he gets bigger. "I will do the same thing."

Does he like his work? "It's okay," he replies. "There's nothing else to do, so it's okay."

Ask Yourself
What words would you use to describe Abdulawal's attitude toward life?

A **UNDERSTANDING THE SELECTION** *Making Connections*

1. Complete the first **four** rows of this chart. Compare and contrast your life with Abdulawal's life. Include at least **one** fact, feeling, or thought for each category.
2. Think of another category you can use to compare your life with his. Add your category to the last row of the chart. Fill in the other two columns for that row.

	You	Abdulawal
Family		
Daily Life		
Responsibilities		
Future		

EXTENDING: If the breadwinner in your family were killed, what role do you think you would play in keeping your family together?

 B **CRITICAL THINKING** *Synthesizing*

1. Imagine that you are a person who is strongly opposed to child labour. Reread the article and underline information that supports that position. Summarize this information in one or two sentences in your notebook.
2. Now imagine that you are a person who thinks that child labour may be necessary in some circumstances. Circle parts of the article that support this position. Summarize this information in one or two sentences in your notebook.
3. What would you do if you knew about cases of child labour in your community or country? Write your thoughts in your notebook.

Synthesizing

- When you synthesize information, you combine bits of information into a complex whole.
- The first step in synthesizing is to **identify** your topic (child labour, for example).
- The second step is to **find** information about your topic in a text or texts.
- The third step is to **think** about **all** the information you have found. Ask yourself: What does this mean? Why is it important? What conclusions can I draw?

C WRITING *An E-Mail Message*

Imagine that Alan Freeman was writing an e-mail message to his eight-year-old son telling him about Abdulawal.

1. Make up a name for the son.
2. Write the message you think Alan would send to his son. Include information that would be interesting to the son.
3. Explain to a partner how the age of your audience influenced the information you included.

> ### TIPS
>
> **Audience**
> - Every time you write, think about how your **audience** (who) will influence the language and tone you use and the content or information you include.
> - Think about **who** you are writing for. A letter to your grandmother will be very different from a letter to your best friend.
>
> **Purpose**
> - Every time you write, think about how your **purpose** (why) will influence the format of your writing.
> - Think about **why** you are writing: do you want to tell someone about your summer plans? Are you trying to give another person instructions or information? Do you want to entertain? Do you want to express your feelings about an event in your life? Will you write a letter, how-to article, report, story, or poem?

D LANGUAGE CONVENTIONS *Quotation Marks*

> - **Quotation marks (" ")** are used to show that someone is speaking.
>   EXAMPLE: "There was nobody else to work in my family."
>
> - If you start with the **speech tag** (telling who is speaking), use a comma before the quotation marks. Use a capital letter on the first word in the quotation.
>   EXAMPLE: He replies, "It's okay."
>
> - If the sentence in quotation marks ends in a question mark, an exclamation mark or period those punctuation marks appear inside the last quotation mark.
>   EXAMPLE: She asked, "When do you work?"
>
> - If the quotation should end in a period, but is followed by a speech tag, use a comma. If the quotation ends in a question mark or an exclamation mark, a comma is not used.
>   EXAMPLE: "I work every day," he replied. "When do you work?" she asked.

1. In your notebook, write **four** lines of dialogue between yourself and Abdulawal. Think about questions you would like to ask him. Invent answers based on the information in the article.
2. Check that you have used quotation marks and placed punctuation marks correctly.

Before Reading

Many of the problems facing the world, such as child labour or war, are complicated and controversial. Many people don't want to get involved in such problems. However, it's usually true that the more complicated the issue, the more your help is needed. The following selection shows one way you can get involved.

How to Write a Petition

INSTRUCTIONS from *Take Action!* by Marc Kielburger and Craig Kielburger

If you are concerned about something, and you think other people share your point of view, you can use a **petition** to gather support for your idea. A petition is a powerful tool for a community. It lets decision-makers know that a lot of people are concerned about a particular issue. It asks them to take action to bring about change.

You can use a petition to help make changes at your school, in your community, or at the municipal, provincial, or federal levels of the government.

FORMAT FOR A PETITION

Give it a title:

To: Who do you want to read your petition? Who can solve the problem?

From: Identify your group. Are you all from the same school or organization?

Purpose: State the reason for submitting a petition. Supply facts to support your submission.

Request: The petition must include a request. What do you want the person(s) receiving the petition to do to solve the problem?

Signatures: Collect as many signatures as you can. Be sure to get a full address beside each name, including city and postal code (if the petition is for your school, than you don't need everyone's address, just homeroom or class).

GOALS AT A GLANCE

identifying sequence • making judgments

Present your petition: Present your petition to a person who will listen to you and who has the power to make changes.

Tip: If there is more than one page to your petition, you must rewrite the purpose and request of the petition at the top of each page.

SAMPLE PETITION

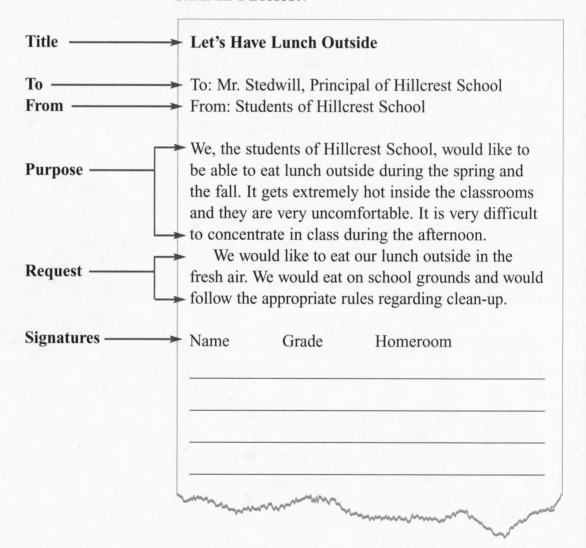

Title → **Let's Have Lunch Outside**

To → To: Mr. Stedwill, Principal of Hillcrest School
From → From: Students of Hillcrest School

Purpose → We, the students of Hillcrest School, would like to be able to eat lunch outside during the spring and the fall. It gets extremely hot inside the classrooms and they are very uncomfortable. It is very difficult to concentrate in class during the afternoon.

Request → We would like to eat our lunch outside in the fresh air. We would eat on school grounds and would follow the appropriate rules regarding clean-up.

Signatures → Name   Grade   Homeroom

_____

_____

_____

_____

HOW TO WRITE A PETITION TO THE FEDERAL GOVERNMENT

In preparing a petition in Canada for the **federal** government, there are **very specific** rules you must follow.

- If you are sending your petition to the federal government, you must submit it to your Member of Parliament (MP) so that it can be read in the House of Commons. Once it has been presented, the government must send a response to the MP within 45 days.

- Petitions can be handwritten, printed, typed, or photocopied on regular-sized paper.

- Always be polite and use appropriate language.

- Be clear and to the point.

- Do not attach anything to the petition.

- The petition must be about an issue the federal government controls. Make sure you send your petition to the right level of government.

- Collect as many signatures as possible. At least 25 signatures are required to have your petition read in the House of Commons.

- The petition must contain a request, called a **prayer**, for Parliament to take some action. A statement of opinion alone will not work. The petition must not demand that Parliament do something.

- Each person who signs the petition must give either a full address or the city and province.

A **UNDERSTANDING THE SELECTION** *Sequencing*

Number the following steps in the order in which they should occur for a petition to be successful:

_____ You present your petition.

_____ You write up your petition.

_____ You become concerned about an issue and decide to do something about it.

_____ You identify the person who can make the change you want.

_____ You decide that a petition is the best way to make the change you want.

_____ You talk to other people to see if they share your concerns about this issue.

_____ You collect as many signatures as you can on your petition.

B **CRITICAL THINKING** *Making Judgments*

According to the selection, a petition can be used to make changes at school, in your community, or at the municipal, provincial, or federal levels of government.

1. Decide which **three** of the following issues you think a petition might help change:

   ❏ hunger around the world
   ❏ cars idling in front of the school
   ❏ stronger gun control laws

   ❏ litter in your schoolyard
   ❏ peace in a nation at war
   ❏ child labour

2. For each issue you chose, identify the person or organization you would send the petition to. Describe the action you would ask for in each case.

Issue	Organization/Person	Action

3. Share and discuss your chart with a small group.

Reflecting

4. What changes, if any, would you make to your chart as a result of the discussion?

_____

_____

WRITING *A Petition*

With a partner or a small group, create a petition on an issue that you think is important. Follow these steps.

1. Talk about issues that you feel are important. Choose one issue that you think could be solved using a petition.
2. Review the information in "How to Write a Petition."
3. Fill in the planner below.

PETITION PLANNER

Title: _____

To: _____

From: _____

Purpose: _____

_____

_____

_____

_____

Request: _____

_____

_____

_____

_____

Printed Name   Signature   Address

_____

4. Make a good copy of your petition on another piece of paper. Add at least 25 lines for signatures.
5. Collect signatures on your petition and send it to the proper person or organization.
6. Report the results of your petition to your class.

7. With your partner or small group, discuss the process you followed to create a petition and collect signatures. What went well? What would you do differently next time?

_____

_____

D LANGUAGE CONVENTIONS *Capital Letters*

- Use a **capital letter** for the first word in a sentence.
  EXAMPLE: She announced the new policy to the crowd.

- Use a **capital letter** for proper nouns (see page 5 for information on proper nouns).
  EXAMPLE: Susan, June, Friday, Labour Day, London

- Use a capital letter for the main words in a title or heading.
  EXAMPLE: Format for a Petition

Add capital letters to the following sentences. Cross out the lower-case letter and write a capital letter above it.

1. we all signed the petition.

2. james and susie are writing a report about the plague in europe.

3. send a copy of the petition to ottawa.

4. my little sister, marie, collected for unicef this halloween.

5. chuck read the story "the vigil" to us.

E MEDIA *In the News*

1. Choose **one** of the issues below:
   - ❏ hunger around the world
   - ❏ gun control laws
   - ❏ peace in a nation at war
   - ❏ child labour
   - ❏ another issue of your choice _____

2. Choose **one** of the following tasks:
   - ❏ View **one** TV program dealing with your issue. In your notebook, list **four** facts or ideas from the program that you think everyone should know.
   - ❏ Read **one** newspaper or magazine article about your issue. In your notebook, list **four** facts or ideas from the article that you think everyone should know.
   - ❏ Find **one** Internet site on your issue. In your notebook, list **four** facts or ideas from the site that you think everyone should know.

3. Write a paragraph summarizing and synthesizing the information you collected.
   Share your paragraph with your class.

Before Reading

What do you think the word **vigil** means? Read this definition and sample sentence:

    vigil: to stay awake for some purpose; watching: <u>All night the father kept **vigil** over</u> <u>the sick child</u>.

Write a prediction for the story based on your understanding of the title.

_____

The Vigil

SHORT STORY by Jan Andrews

Caitlin Roberts and her brother Kevin dashed along the dirt road that led through their small, Newfoundland village, past the church and down onto the beach. For a moment they stood together throwing pebbles through the mist and drizzle out into the calm, flat, greyness of the sea drinking in the quiet and freedom of an early Saturday morning. Then they were off again, heading for the high, rough arm of land that led on into the next <u>cove</u> in the coastline of Bonavista Bay. They scrambled to the top, two slight, <u>wiry</u> figures of about the same height, both ruggedly dressed in windbreakers, blue jeans, and rubber boots.

> **VOCABULARY**
>
> **cove**: a small, sheltered bay
> **wiry**: lean and strong

GOALS AT A GLANCE

recalling details • making inferences

A lock of Caitlin's long, black hair fell across her face. As she pushed it back, her grey eyes widened.

"Kev," she cried, pointing ahead, "look!"

What she had seen sped them on. Within seconds they were running, as hard as they could, down to where a huge, black shape lay stranded on the beach.

"A whale," Kevin called. As he spoke, his boot kicked at a broad line of small, dead fish, thrown up along the high water mark. "Must have come after the caplin," he panted.

The two of them were close to the great creature now. Their coming had alarmed it. It began to thrash and churn about. Stones and sand and spray were flung up from where the outgoing tide lapped around its tail. Its body writhed and twisted, carving deep into the seabed. Its fins flapped as if, in some dreadful way, it was trying to walk. They stood back, watching in horror.

Ask Yourself
Why do Kevin and Caitlin feel "horror" at what they see?

"It won't get off, will it?" Caitlin said bleakly, so the words made a statement rather than a question.

Kevin shook his dark, curly head. "No," he answered. "Remember, up by Twillingate, last year. There was a beached whale. It was on TV. Folks came from St. John's even, trying to push it off. But it wasn't any good. The whale died."

"Let's go somewhere else," Caitlin suggested.

He bent, picked up a stone, weighed it in his hand and let it drop. The whale thrashed still more desperately. Air came sighing and steaming out of its blowhole. A long, shuddering, heaving breath was sucked back in.

Kevin nodded in agreement. They moved on up the beach, walking quickly at first, their boots clumping against the shift and rattle of pebbles, their hands thrust deep into their jacket pockets. Then gradually, their steps slowed. They stopped here and there to poke in pretended interest at driftwood and shells and seaweed. A glance passed between them. Kevin looked over his shoulder and, with one accord, they turned back.

Ask Yourself
Why do you think Caitlin and Kevin turn back?

"Walk gently this time, eh?" Caitlin whispered. Again Kevin took up a stone and again he let it drop. The whale seemed exhausted. It was eyeing them warily through its tiny, deep-set eyes but, though its body almost quivered with tension, it lay still. They moved quietly nearer.

They had almost reached the place where they had stood before when they realized that, out between the rocks at the cove's mouth, other whales were appearing. A steam-spout thrust upward and then another. Four dark, enormous shapes rose magnificently from the water, arced through the mist and plunged.

"They've come to be with it," Kevin said. "I've heard of that."

"Shh," Caitlin commanded. "Listen!"

From the blowhole of the whale on the beach a strange, high sound soared. It was answered by a succession of wavering notes. And again the four shapes rose, this time close in to the shore. Squeaks and cries and long drawn whistles thrilled electric onto the grey, cold morning air.

"It's like they're talking to each other," Caitlin said in <u>awe</u>.

Suddenly, she realized her cheeks were wet with tears. She looked at the creature on the beach and then out into the cove. Beside her, there came a small choked-back sob. Turning, she saw that Kevin was crying too. He wiped his hand slowly across his eyes.

"They'll stay now till it's dead, won't they?" Caitlin asked through the lump in her throat.

"Yes! Yes, of course!"

As the communication between the whales went on, Kevin perched himself against a rock.

"Will you mind Cat?" he said at last.

"Mind what?"

"When it's dead and Dad and the men come to cut it. I saw that on TV too. There's a wonderful lot of meat on a whale."

© Gage Learning Corporation

Caitlin hung her head to let her black hair shut out her vision for a while. "Sort of," she answered quietly. "But…but it would only rot and stink otherwise, like the caplin."

"What if…?"

The harshness in her brother's voice made her glance up quickly. His round, usually cheerful, face was pale and stained.

"What if what?" she asked.

"Well…well if there'd been a gang of us, say. See… see it would have been different. We'd have yelled and laughed and someone would've thrown a stone. Someone would've, sure to. Then we'd all have done it. It wouldn't have been like it is now. It wouldn't, would it? Not at all! No way!"

The worry in Caitlin's grey eyes <u>acknowledged</u> the truth of his statement. He looked at his watch.

"Some other kid is bound to come here before long," he said. "Soon as one knows, they all will."

"We'll have to stay here then."

"We'll have to guard it, all day if need be."

"But…"

"Cat, we're not enough. What if the Riley boys come? There's five and they're all so big. They won't listen to us."

"We need help, a grown up."

"Yeah, but…well everyone's got something going Saturday and…"

"Not the teacher. Saturday's his day off. And Mr. Jones is nice all right."

"We can't both go, Cat."

"I'll go. OK?"

"OK."

Kevin hesitated. "Cat," he said. "We're not being <u>daft</u>, are we? I mean…I mean it's only an old whale and it's going to die, for sure, anyway."

Doubt crept into Caitlin's mind. Already the drizzle was soaking through her jeans and running down her neck. She could feel the beginnings of cold and hunger, and fear of what the other kids in the village would say.

"I don't know," she muttered.

The whale on the beach let out another of its high, strange cries. Once more the cry was answered. Brother and sister looked at one another. They knew then that, just as before they had not been able to walk away, so they would not be able to walk away now.

"We've got to, haven't we?" Caitlin whispered.

Kevin nodded. Resolutely, he made for the worn track back to the village; resolutely Caitlin squared her thin shoulders and planted her feet and took up her position at the whale's side. It breathed, shuddered, breathed again.

"We've got to," Caitlin told herself. "And… and we will!"

* * * * * *

So it was, that with the watching of Caitlin and Kevin Roberts and the help and authority of Mr. Jones on land, and with the companionship of its fellows waiting and calling to it from the sea, the whale on the beach came to the moment of its death with peace. Gentle then was its passing; gentle and calm like a cloud moving across the sun and breaking up and disappearing on a summer's day; certain as the tide that rose to wash healing and salt and cold around it. For the first time, Caitlin put out a hand to touch the great body.

"The men'll come tomorrow, won't they?" she said softly. "They'll cut it. It'll be all a mess, then nothing."

Kevin reached over and touched the dead animal too. "I won't be sorry we stayed," he said. "Not ever."

Caitlin took a last look out into the cove. Somehow she could feel that already the other whales were swimming past the rocks and out into the open and away.

"No more will I," she said firmly. "No more will either of us."

Ask Yourself
Why do you think Kevin and Caitlin only touch the whale when it is dead?

A CRITICAL THINKING *Making Inferences*

As you answer the following questions, put yourself in the place of the characters. Think about why they behave as they do.

1. How do Caitlin and Kevin feel when the whales in the water begin to communicate with the beached whale?

   _____

   _____

2. Why do Caitlin and Kevin think they would have acted differently towards the whale if they had been with other kids?

   _____

   _____

3. Does the whale die in the way Caitlin and Kevin hope it will? Explain.

   _____

   _____

EXTENDING: In your response journal, write about the problems Caitlin and Kevin face and the decisions they make. Explain how you would have behaved in the same situation.

B UNDERSTANDING THE SELECTION *Recalling Details*

Circle the best answer for each multiple-choice question.

1. Where do Caitlin and Kevin live?
   a. on the beach　　　　　　　　**b.** along the dirt road
   c. in a small Newfoundland village　**d.** on a boat

2. How does the beached whale react when Caitlin and Kevin approach it?
   a. It pushes rotting caplin at them.　**b.** It thrashes and churns about.
   c. It sounds an alarm.　　　　　　**d.** It calls the other whales.

3. How do the whales in the water communicate with the whale on the beach?
   a. They whistle and squeak.　　　**b.** They jump out of the water.
   c. They come to be with it.　　　　**d.** None of the above.

4. What does Kevin say will probably happen to the whale after it dies?
   a. It will wash away in the tide.　　**b.** It will rot and stink.
   c. People will cut it up for meat.　　**d.** Other kids will throw rocks at it.

C ORAL COMMUNICATION *Retelling the Story*

1. Imagine that you are Caitlin or Kevin 15 years after this story takes place. You want to tell your children what happened with the whale on the beach.
2. What will you tell them about the events that day? How will you describe your thoughts and feelings? Make some notes about what you would like to say.
3. **Retell** this story to a partner in role as the older Caitlin or Kevin.
4. Compare your version of the story with your partner's. How do you account for the differences? Write your thoughts in your notebook.

> To **retell** means to tell a story in a new way to someone.

D VOCABULARY *Compound Words*

> • A **compound word** is a word that is made up of two or more words. Compound words sometimes have a **hyphen (-)**.
>
> EXAMPLE: blowhole, somehow, coastline, together, narrow-minded
>
> • You can sometimes figure out the meaning of the compound word by thinking about the meanings of the individual words.
>
> EXAMPLE: **blow** + **hole** = a <u>hole</u> through which a whale <u>blows</u> air and breathes

1. Figure out the meaning of each <u>underlined</u> compound word by thinking about the meanings of the individual words that make up the compound. Write the meaning of the compound word in the space provided.

   a. Caitlin and Kevin watch the waves crashing on the <u>coastline</u> of the bay.

   _____

   b. They stop here and there along the beach to poke at <u>driftwood</u>.

   _____

   c. The <u>outgoing</u> tide laps around the tail of the whale.

   _____

   d. The whale eyes them through its tiny, <u>deep-set</u> eyes.

   _____

   e. Caitlin and Kevin want to save the whale from the <u>hard-hearted</u> village boys.

   _____

2. In your notebook, write a sentence using each compound word below:

   inland   wetsuit   overseas   narrow-minded   shortcut

> • A **contraction** is a word formed by joining two other words. An **apostrophe (')** takes the place of the missing letters.
>   EXAMPLES: was + not = wasn't   will + not = won't

1. Underline the contractions in the sentences below. In the space provided, write the words that have been combined.

   a. Let's go somewhere else. _____

   b. We're not enough. _____

   c. For sure someone would've thrown a stone. _____

   d. There's a wonderful lot of meat on a whale. _____

   e. What if there'd been a gang of us? _____

   f. The teacher, he'd keep them away. _____

   g. The men'll come tomorrow. _____

2. Complete the conversation below, using at least **five** contractions.

   Mother: What have you two been up to today?

   Caitlin: _____

   Kevin: _____

   Mother: _____

   Caitlin: _____

   Kevin: _____

   Mother: _____

   Kevin: _____

   Caitlin: _____

TIPS

Contractions
- Contractions make your writing sound informal.
- You can use contractions in dialogue. But do not use contractions in formal writing: reports and essays.
- Look at some of your recent writing. If you have used contractions, check that you used them correctly. Is the apostrophe in the right place?

UNIT 6 WRAP-UP

SELF-ASSESSMENT *Critical Thinking Strategies*

1. In your notebook, explain how you used at least **three** of the following critical thinking strategies. How did they improve your understanding of the selections?

   ❏ identifying main events
   ❏ making inferences
   ❏ making connections
   ❏ synthesizing
   ❏ making judgments

2. Set a personal goal for using and improving your use of the above strategies. Explain what you will do.

PROJECT IDEA *Action Plan*

Put some of the ideas in this unit to work and get involved in your community! Create an action plan to solve a problem in your school or community. To complete this project, work with at least three other classmates.

Step 1. With your group, discuss some of the problems or issues in your school or community. Together, choose **one** problem you would all like to solve.

Step 2. Brainstorm some ideas for solving the problem. Think about how you can use the following: personal narratives or articles about the problem, surveys, petitions, e-mail messages, or posters. What else can you try?

Step 3. Have each group member choose **one** idea to work on independently **or** work on at least **four** ideas as a group. Write down an action plan, explaining what you plan to do.

Step 4. Before you begin the tasks on your action plan, share the plan with your teacher or another adult. Ask for advice or assistance if necessary.

Step 5. Get started. Depending on your plan, it may take a few days, weeks, or months before you see any results. Keep in touch with other group members to let them know what you're doing.

Step 6. Meet with your group to discuss the results of your action plan. If your plan was successful, congratulate each other. If your plan didn't get you what you wanted, talk about other things you can try. What worked and what didn't work? What did you learn from the things you did try?

When you <u>synthesize</u> information, you combine bits of information into a complex whole. To synthesize you may need to summarize (see page 45) information. Synthesizing can help you make connections (page 135) and draw conclusions (page 92).

Note Facts

The story "The Vigil" gives you the following facts about beached whales:
- The children have seen another beached whale on TV.
- The beached whale is helpless and cannot get back to water.
- Other whales swim nearby and call to the whale.

Draw Conclusions

From those facts the following conclusions about beached whales could be synthesized:
- Whales do get beached (it's happened before in another community).
- A beached whale will die.
- Other whales will keep the dying whale company.

Synthesize

Those conclusions could be synthesized into a more complex whole:
- When a whale is beached, other whales will keep it company until it dies.

Check

Since "The Vigil" is a short story, you will want to check its facts with nonfiction sources. You might do an Internet search for newspaper articles using the key words
beached whales + news.

You will certainly discover that many whales get beached every year. However, you may also find out that sometimes it's possible to rescue beached whales. You may also discover that none of the news articles mention other whales calling to the beached whale.

Ask yourself: What does all of this mean? Why are these bits of information important? What conclusions can I draw?

NEXT TIME

The next time you read a selection, think about its facts. Make connections to other facts in that selection, other texts, and your own knowledge. Draw conclusions. Combine the bits of information into one big picture.

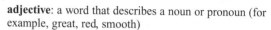

GLOSSARY

adjective: a word that describes a noun or pronoun (for example, great, red, smooth)

adverb: a word that modifies a verb, an adjective, or another adverb. It tells the reader more about the action (for example, slowly, brightly)

audience: anyone who will be reading your writing

brainstorm: to contribute ideas on one topic in a group

cause and effect: when one event makes another event happen

collage: a picture made by arranging items with different colours, textures, and shapes on a background

comma: a punctuation mark (**,**) that separates elements in a sentence and tells the reader to pause

command: a statement or phrase that orders you to do something (for example: Get me my coat.)

compound sentence: two complete sentences joined by a conjunction

compound word: a word made up of two or more words (for example, headache, room-mate)

conclusion: the section of a piece of writing that sums up earlier information

conjunction: a word (for example, and, but, because) that is used to join words or groups of words

context: the words or sentences around a word that help to show its meaning

contraction: a word formed by joining two other words with an apostrophe (for example, **she's** meaning "she is")

definition: an explanation of what a word means

dialogue: the words characters speak to each other

draw conclusions: to use information in the text to make decisions about the characters or events

entry word: a word in a dictionary that shows the spelling of a word and divides it into syllables

exclamation: a sentence or phrase that expresses strong feeling (for example: Help!)

exclamation mark: a punctuation mark (**!**) that shows a sentence is an exclamation

flowchart: a diagram that clearly shows the order of a series of events in a story or article, or the steps in a process

homophone: a word that sounds the same as another word or words, but has a different meaning and a different spelling (for example, its, it's)

idiom: an expression with a meaning different from the dictionary definition of its individual words (for example, he has a chip on his shoulder)

infer (make inferences): to use clues in the text or "read between the lines" to make an educated guess about what is happening in the text

information paragraph: a paragraph that organizes facts or knowledge about a topic

jargon: the language of a particular group or profession, which is often difficult for an outsider to understand

KWL chart: a chart recording what you **K**now, **W**ant to Know, and have **L**earned

noun: a word that names a person, place, thing, quality, or event

period: a punctuation mark (**.**) that ends a statement or command

personal narrative: a piece of writing that describes an important event in a writer's life. It answers the questions **who, what, where, when, why,** and **how.**

possessive form: using an apostrophe (**'**), usually followed by the letter **-s**, to show ownership

possessive pronouns: words that show ownership of something (for example, mine, hers, its). Some possessive pronouns act as adjectives (for example, their, your).

predict: to make an educated guess before or during reading about what will happen in a text

present tense: the verb tense that is used to tell what is happening now, or that an action is ongoing

pronoun: a word used in place of a noun (for example, me, you, I)

pronunciation key: the code in a dictionary that tells you how to say a word

proper noun: a word that names a particular person, place, or thing, and begins with a capital letter (for example, Nancy, Vancouver, Nunavut)

purpose: the reason a text was created (for example, to persuade someone to do or buy something)

question: a sentence that asks something (for example: Where should we go?)

question mark: the punctuation mark (**?**) used to end a question.

quotation marks: punctuation marks (**" "**) that are used to show that someone is speaking

retell: to tell a story in a new way

root: a word or part of a word that can be used to form other words (for example, un**comfort**able)

scene: one part or section of a play, set in one location

sentence fragment: a group of words that looks like a sentence but does not express a complete thought

sequel: a story that continues from where another story finishes

skim: to quickly read parts of a text to get a sense of what it is about

slogan: a short, easy-to-remember message

speech tag: words that come before or after dialogue to show who is speaking

statement: a sentence or phrase that tells you something

summarize: to make a brief statement giving the main points of the text

supporting details: facts, examples, or experiences that back up your topic sentence

synonym: a word that means the same thing or almost the same thing as another word (for example, bawled, cried, wailed)

synthesizing: combining bits of information into a complex whole

tense: the tense of a verb tells the time (past, present, or future) of the action, feeling, or state of being

topic sentence: a statement that tells what a piece of writing is about

Venn diagram: a chart that uses two overlapping circles to show differences and similarities between two items

verb: a word that expresses an action, feeling, or state of bei

vivid verbs: strong descriptive action words (for exampl bellowed)

INDEX

Bold numbers indicate Strategy
boxes and Close-Up pages.